A Profile
in Joy

A Profile
in Joy

The Life of Stephen Kim

ANNA BELLE LAUGHBAUM

Nazarene Publishing House
Kansas City, Missouri

To Grace

whose name describes her well
in her devotion to God, Stephen, and family,
and who is an important part of this book

CONTENTS

ANNA BELLE LAUGHBAUM, Ph.D., is a former professor of English at Southern Nazarene University, Bethany, Okla. She has also served in this capacity at Seattle Pacific University, Korea Nazarene Theological College, and European Nazarene Bible College.

Dr. Laughbaum has authored numerous articles for Christian periodicals, and two prior adult NWMS reading books, *Branches of the Vine* and *Korea, I Will Always Remember Your Grace.*

PREFACE

A *Profile in Joy* is the story of a young Korean who walked through the valley of the shadow of death and emerged a conqueror. It is also the story of three diverse cultures, the impact of their diversity on a fledgling ministry, and the positive result of cross-cultural experience. Finally, it is the story of compassionate ministries and their far-reaching influence on one young life.

I became acquainted with Kim Sung Kap, better known as Stephen, in 1982 when I taught at Korea Nazarene Theological College in Ch'onan City, Korea. Stephen was a student there, editor of the campus newspaper, and a leader on campus. When I returned home in 1983, we corresponded and kept in touch until his death in 1991.

When I approached Stephen about writing his biography, I did not hear from him for some time. Finally, he wrote and said that he did not feel "qualified" to have a book written about him but had been praying about it. "After days of prayer," he said, "I can say, 'Praise the Lord!' This is a wonderful plan of God."

"If people knew my biography was being written," he wrote, "they would probably laugh. They'd say, 'How old are you? A biography written about one so young?' I can only answer like this: 'I haven't lived long but God has allowed me to live much, much more.'"

Stephen continued, "My prayer for this book is that all the readers will get a vivid picture of how God is fulfilling His divine purpose in me. He promised me that I would be 'known, yet regarded as unknown; dying, and yet [I] live on; beaten, and yet not killed; sorrowful, yet always rejoicing; poor, yet making many rich; having nothing and yet possessing everything'" (2 Cor. 6:9-10).

I laughed and cried, marveled and rejoiced as Stephen told me about his life. He always called me "Mom." "I have been calling you 'Ma'am,'" he said. "I think now I'll call you 'Mom.' If you were here in the Philippines, people would surely call you 'Mom' out of respect."

"Mom, I must be open with you," Stephen said many times as he talked about himself. "Open," to him, meant to be frank and not hide anything. "I want to pour out everything just as it is. I don't want to exaggerate anything. Even my shortcomings I'd like to talk about." He wanted me to know that some things he would tell me were "shameful." That word often means "embarrassing"; sometimes it really does mean "shameful." "I must be truthful" introduced more than one episode or experience he discussed. I believe he was.

It wasn't always easy for Stephen to talk about himself, his family, his graduate studies, or his ministry. He realized, he said, how far short he fell in modeling an exemplary student, husband, and minister. "I must confess to you," he explained, "how many times I have wanted to stop talking about my life. The person in the book should be a model, a good model of the Christian life—in all things. I am struggling with immaturity. I don't think I am a very good model. But when I wanted to stop telling about my life, God encouraged me time and time again to continue."

In an important sense, *A Profile in Joy* is an autobiography. Stephen suggested several areas of his life that were most meaningful to him and talked informally about them. As he talked, he commented on topics that were not relevant to the one being discussed but certainly relevant to his life and thought. One of my roles was that of organizer.

For the most part, I have used the words of Stephen and his wife, Grace, with attempts to clarify and fill in gaps.

"You know, Mom, my English is limited," Stephen told me over and over again.

Stephen's prayer for this book is that readers will see the way God works out His plan in the life of the believer. May his prayer be answered! May also Stephen's challenges, his conquering spirit in the face of adversity, and his love of life and service inspire and challenge every reader.

—ANNA BELLE LAUGHBAUM

ACKNOWLEDGMENTS

I am indebted to the following friends of Stephen and give grateful thanks for their writing about him: Dr. Jim Edlin, professor of theology at MidAmerica Nazarene College and former academic dean and professor at Asia-Pacific Nazarene Theological Seminary; Dr. E. LeBron Fairbanks, president of Mount Vernon Nazarene College and former president of APNTS; Rev. Tim Mercer, missionary to Korea and professor of theology at Korea Nazarene Theological College; Dr. Donald Owens, general superintendent and former missionary to Korea, Asia-Pacific regional director, and president of APNTS; Dr. William Patch, former president of KNTC, and Gail Patch, professor of English; Dr. Kenneth Pearsall, president emeritus of Northwest Nazarene College and former interim president of KNTC; Dr. George Rench, Asia-Pacific regional director; Dr. Roy Stults, editor of *World Mission* magazine, former professor of theology at APNTS, and former professor at KNTC.

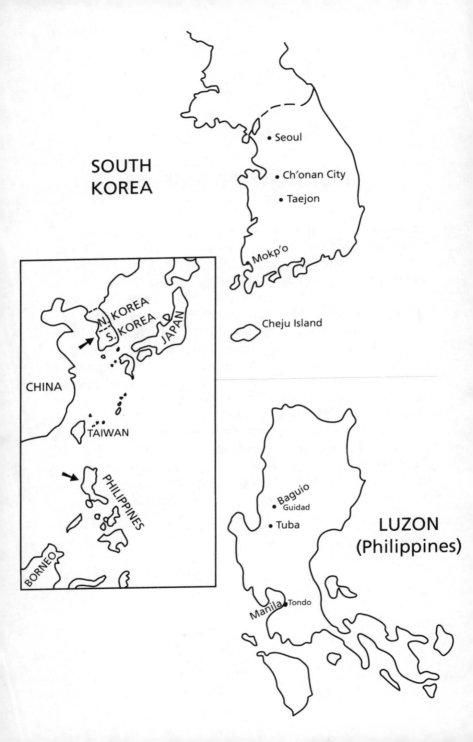

1

A PROFILE OF STEPHEN

Dr. Donald Owens wrote this tribute to Stephen: Whatever is written about Kim Sung Kap, or Stephen Kim as he is known among our American and Filipino community, one can only say that he is a profile in courage and joy. Stephen was born in the home of a minister's family in the port city of Mokp'o on the southern coast of the Korean peninsula. In the midst of his family's poverty and struggle to build a church in that city, Stephen had the added sorrow of being crippled with polio. When I first saw him and visited his home in Mokp'o, I was impressed by his lack of fear to engage in conversation with the missionaries as he exercised his growing power in the English language. With tears in his eyes, Stephen's father pleaded with the missionaries to help provide a way into ministry for his son upon whom the hand of adversity had fallen so hard.

I saw in Stephen Kim an electrifying courage and determination to make his life an offering of praise and servanthood to Christ. He knew that through his mastery of the English language, doors would be opened for him to serve. He attempted everything with vigor, enthusiasm, and joy. He simply believed that nothing would be impossible for him.

In Korea Nazarene Theological College, Stephen excelled in his studies and contributed greatly to the spiritual tenor of the institution by his joy, courage, and faith. He developed a particular fondness for Dr. Anna Belle Laughbaum, who ministered very effectively in the college for two years. This fellowship and loving relationship between Dr. Laughbaum, Stephen Kim and his wife, Grace, continued even after Dr. Laughbaum's tenure at KNTC was completed.

Throughout his studies in the Philippines at Asia-Pacific Nazarene Theological Seminary, again the virtues of courage and joy, along with the determination to excel, characterized his life. His wholesome and wonderful attitude spread joy throughout the institution. Again the hand of difficulty lay heavily upon him when he fought a battle with a brain tumor. In goodness and grace God helped Stephen Kim through that experience as well as an effective pastorate in the Church of the Nazarene in Baguio in the Philippines. God blessed him and Grace with beautiful children. During the devastating earthquake that wrought such destruction in that part of the Philippine Islands, Stephen maximized the use of contacts among Koreans and other associates to bring relief to the battered community.

Nobility, courage, and great joy . . . a profile of Stephen Kim.

Stephen Kim and Anna Belle Laughbaum

2

FAMILY SNAPSHOT

First, Mom, I'd like to tell you some things about me, and then I want to talk about the members of my family.

When my father was pastoring in the rural area, I was born at my uncle's house in Mokp'o. It was a restaurant at that time. I was born the third son, but if you include my sister (she was the first child in our family), I was the fourth child. It used to be that just the sons were counted, but that is changing.

I was a normal boy until I was three years old. I was the beloved of my parents and of many other people. I was handsome and clever; this is what I was told. One day both of my legs were paralyzed. I could not walk or stand or even sit. My parents took me to the hospital. The doctors gave no hope. My parents spent much money trying to help me. My father's life really went down financially. I can still remember that my mother always carried me. She carried me to church and was continually crying. Her tears dropped on my face, and I cried with her. I remember the time she carried me to an acupuncturist for a medical treatment. My parents tried so many things, but I was still a crippled boy.

After two years like this, I remember the morning my father came from the prayer mountain. He said, "Son, I want to pray for you." He and my mother were both holding me. My father laid his hands on my head and my legs. Then they prayed with tears, "Lord, please let him walk."

Suddenly I was able to stretch out my two legs—they couldn't move before—and I was able to sit and stand and walk. God really healed me! Even though I limped in my right leg, I could walk. God answered my parents' prayers.

Mokp'o

My first healing was physical. My second healing was spiritual. It happened February 23, 1980. I was really struggling with God, for even though my father was a pastor and I was a P.K., I had not met the Lord personally. I was very active in the church. Always, I thought, I must do my duty. Everything I did in the church was an obligation. I was brought up this way. I was always thinking, "Why do I have to do it? Why am I doing it?" I had no peace in my heart.

So I fasted and prayed for seven days, and this was the last day. Then the second miracle of healing took place. It cannot be compared with the first miracle, for it was much greater. Our physical condition is not forever, but our spiritual life is eternal. I accepted the Lord as my personal Savior. My life was changed. Before I met the Lord I was very selfish. I thought first of me. But God changed my life completely. Now I was God-centered and others-centered.

For instance, at Asia-Pacific Nazarene Theological Seminary, Grace and I had very little money. Because of our medical expenses sometimes we had only a few pesos for jeepney fare. One time we had only 500 pesos that we planned to use for rice and other food. But that evening we saw a Filipino friend who was suffering from lack of nutrition. He was eating just one meal a day. God inspired us to give that money to our friend. We prayed and then gave him the whole amount. I never would have done that before God changed my selfish behavior. Do you know what, Mom? Soon after we gave that money, God provided rice for us.

Grace's parents noticed another big change in us when they came to Baguio when Paul was born. They could not understand why we had no desire for money or possessions or why we had peace in our hearts and were content even though we had almost nothing. Almost every day they were advising Grace and me to prepare for our future. We told them, "Everything in our future is in God's hands, and He will provide for us. We want to live God-centered lives." Grace's mother accepted the Lord through our prayers and family devotions. She could see God in our lives.

When I was quite young, I had three wishes. The first was to go on picnics when I was in elementary school. We had two, one in summer and one in autumn. Until the sixth grade I could not join my classmates in them. I envied them. How happy I was when I was able to go with them. My second wish was to ride a bicycle. You remember, Mom, I rode one when I was at KNTC. My third wish was to ride in a helicopter. That wish was fulfilled in July 1990 as a result of the earthquake in the Philippines.

American army men at Clark Air Force Base used helicopters to deliver people from Baguio to Manila. I was one of those people. It was a *big* helicopter!

Of course, throughout my life I have had many other more important desires. God has granted many of them. One was to attend Korea Nazarene Theological Seminary. God provided, and good things happened there. One thing that happened I am hesitant to talk about, but I must be open with you. I added three years to my age. My Korean friends think I am 31 years old, but my real age is 28. This is how it happened. Korean culture is very much an age-centered culture. People want to be older than they are because they receive more respect this way. The first thing we want to know when we are introduced to a new friend is his age. That's why in our country it is permissible to ask a lady her age. We want to know how old she is so we can give her more respect.

Unfortunately, I lost my true age when I was at KNTC. I courted Grace then. She was 22 years old. I was only 19. So I added three years to my age. My calendar age is 28, but what about my spiritual age? With God's help I can be more spiritually mature and not be bound by my calendar age.

Now I will tell you about my family. First, my grandmother. She was really a beautiful Christian. She had three sons and two daughters. One daughter passed away. My father is the middle son. During her later years, my grandmother lived in my father's house. When I came home on vacation from KNTC, I enjoyed seeing her. Always when I saw her she asked me to go to the church sanctuary with her. She prayed for me there.

One time after she prayed for me, she looked at me. Her eyes penetrated my face. She said, "Stephen, I cannot see the Spirit of God. I cannot see the fire." To her "fire" meant the Spirit of God. This embarrassed me. The next time I went home I took some candy. Grandmother really liked candy, so I took several packs. I wanted to hear from her that I had "fire" on my face. I gave them to her and she was very happy. After she prayed she said, "Stephen, thank you for this candy. You really love me. But there is no fire on your face." I was really embarrassed this time.

Grandmother always went to early morning prayer meeting. In Korea all the churches have prayer meetings about 4:30 A.M. Grandmother prayed during those meetings for all her grandchildren and great-grandchildren, who numbered 23 at that time. She prayed for us one by one. Grandmother called on the old people around the church. When they came to church she would preach to them, "Believe in Jesus. This is the only way, the only hope we old people can hold." In her Korean Bible there is hardly any space left, for she was always writing in it whatever inspired her. She memorized much of the Bible. I have it now. It is a great remembrance of her.

My grandmother loved to sing. I heard from my family that when she was younger and the pastor did not know the number of the hymn he wanted to sing, he asked my grandmother, "Mrs. Kim, where is this hymn?" She always told him. She sang with a slow tune, a slow melody. She could not hear very well, so did not always know what stanza the congregation was singing. If the hymn had four stanzas everybody else finished before she did. Still she was singing on the third stanza. Everybody had to wait until she finished and then my father would continue the service.

I remember my grandmother as a person of prayer, a person of the Word of God, and a person of praise, worship, and evangelism. Her life influenced all of us children, grandchildren, and great-grandchildren. When she passed away, there was no question but what she was in heaven. We really believed that. She was the model of the Christian life.

I have four brothers and a sister. My sister is the oldest child in our family. Young Min Kim is really a beautiful girl. I cannot forget how much she helped me when I was in middle school. She influenced me a lot in eloquence. She encouraged me to enter contests in oratory. I lost the first seven contests. Each time I was discouraged and didn't want to try again. But Young Min always told me, "Try again." I won the eighth contest and many more. I participated in several important competitions in Korea.

My eldest brother, Elijah, is a pastor in Seoul. He has had a great, great influence upon me. I wrote a poem about him.

Country Man

His pronunciation is not so clear
He has been eating dog meat
A strange man
Eleven-thirty at night
Writing a prayer letter
To younger brother Stephen
Holding the Lord's bleeding hands.

I have experienced
Many miracles through his prayers
Yet questioning myself
Why this man
He moved God's hands.

Where he is living
Ka Kak Dong a portion of Seoul
I in Baguio a mountain province
Distance cannot stop his prayers
True love he has for his brother.

In his letter advising me that
I have to be ready
To give up myself
For the sake of the ministry
That's not the point
I ridiculed him
Yet I was deeply impressed.

A mighty man of mighty God
Sharp in the Word of God
Memorizing so much Scripture
Stephen my beloved one
Shouting with tears
Moving the throne of God.

Healed through his prayer
Wanting to relax, to be lazy
No Stephen God healed you
Because of prayer
Keep the altar at your knees
Painful order from him.

Right
Visitation will start tomorrow
Bible study restarting
I am willing
To fully commit myself
For the kingdom of God.

Yes younger brother
Gives praise that
This country man's heart
Loves and embraces him.

On Kap, my younger brother, has one boy, Jung Man.
My youngest brother, Ku Kap, has a boy, Jung Moo. Ku
Kap was always very frank. Our family would have a
conference about once a month. My parents were there.
My eldest brother was emcee. We shared experiences. My
youngest brother was always complaining, "Why is
everyone ordering me to do things? I'm not your servant. I
am tired of this." But now he's different, he's helpful. He's
big physically, the biggest guy in my family.

I'm very close to my sisters-in-law, especially the
wives of my eldest and elder brothers. They took care of
me, we shared burdens and prayed for each other.

Mom, I want to say something about the children in my brothers' and sister's families and in my own. My elder brother has a boy and a girl. My sister has two boys and a girl. I have a boy and a girl. Only my elder brother has no boys, just two girls. Sometimes he's quite sad because he has no boys. In Korea the feeling is still strong for families to have more boys than girls. This is due to our cultural background influenced by 1,000 years of Confucianism and 500 years of Buddhism. Boys are needed to take care of their parents when they are old. Our country is a boy-centered culture still.

Now Grace will talk about herself and her family:

I was born January 20, 1959, in Ch'unch'on, just an hour by bus to Ch'onan City. When I was five years old my parents moved to Seoul. I remained with my grandparents. I was to live with my grandparents just until my parents got settled in Seoul. However, I stayed with them until I graduated from high school. After I finished middle school I planned to enter high school in Seoul, but my mother passed away about then.

A year after my mother's death, we accepted our step-mother. It was very difficult for me to adjust to the life of my stepmother. My father was very strict and did not try to understand his children. My younger brother was the eldest son in the family. He died during his first year in high school. That was the biggest sorrow in my family since my mother died.

I tried to live with my stepmother and my father. But I missed my grandmother. I worried about her because she was alone. My grandfather had passed away. So I lived with her and graduated from high school in Ch'unch'on. Then I moved to Ch'onan City where I got a job.

Until this time I had no opportunity to meet our Lord. I remember the time I became acquainted with Him. It was in the autumn of 1978. A Nazarene steward lived in front of my house. She is now the wife of a Nazarene elder in the Ch'onan Church of the Nazarene. She witnessed to me and invited me to church. I went with her one Wednesday night to prayer meeting. That's how I started to attend the Nazarene church. Later in Ch'onan City, I went to the church where Stephen and I were married and where he was associate pastor while he was at KNTC.

That same year, in the wintertime, God graciously came into my heart, and I dedicated myself fully to Him. That was a life-changing experience for me. My younger sisters and brothers began attending church too. And on Easter Sunday my younger brother, my younger sister, and I were baptized. But my father did not want us to attend church. My brother and sister had to obey my father's desire and were hesitant about going to church. But for me my biggest priority was my faith in God. I didn't want anyone to rob me of it or to block my Christian path. That's why sometimes there was trouble between my parents and me. But I felt that I must go to church where I could have a place to pray, cry, and pour out my heart. When my boss wanted me to work on Sunday, I told him I must go to church Sunday morning, but after the service I would work.

One morning the pastor talked about Korea Nazarene Theological College in Ch'onan City. He said, "Those who are willing to be full-time workers for God should think about going there." Right at that time it seemed that was God's calling for me. My heart was beating fast, and I could not breathe very well. I could not understand what was happening. I began praying, "Lord, it seems like it is impossible for me to go to this college. My father wouldn't want me to go. I just accepted You a few months ago, and I don't know how to read the Bible or pray. And what about the financial need?"

But I continued to pray about KNTC. I prayed consistently for one year. I could not counsel with my parents or other family members. Even in the church there were only a few people I could counsel with. I took the entrance examination in Seoul, with a prayer in my heart words cannot express. It was a secret prayer between God and me.

At home I waited for the results of the examination. Then I received a letter of acceptance from KNTC. I had a little money I had saved from working, so I was able to survive the first year, but from the second year on I had a hard time. I did receive an academic scholarship. Because of it I was able to continue until I graduated. There were nine girls in my freshman class. By the time I graduated eight had dropped out. So I was the only girl in my class.

It was my first year during winter vacation that I was courted by my classmate, Stephen. That was a great experience! He took care of me, and we prayed together. At this time I was living at home. I would arrive at the campus about an hour before my first class. I went to the chapel and prayed for myself, for Stephen, and about the vision God had given to us about working in His kingdom. We wanted to prepare ourselves well.

When I was a junior in 1982 we were engaged, and the next year, May 2, 1983, we were married in the church we were serving. On February 23, 1984, Stephen and I graduated, with the blessings of all the people and our thanksgiving to the Lord. A few months later we left Korea for the Philippines to attend Asia-Pacific Nazarene Theological Seminary in Manila.

3

A LASTING INFLUENCE

Before I entered elementary school, my parents were faced with an important decision—whether they would put me in a special school for the handicapped or in a regular school. They were really thinking of me. First of all, they knew if they put me in a special school, there would be many advantages. However, my mother believed that I should go to a regular school. She said I would be with normal people all of my life, so I must learn to overcome my fears and think about being somebody. So I entered San Jung Elementary School.

I praise my Lord that I did go there, for a very wonderful thing happened when I was in the third grade. This was in 1970. I had a beautiful Christian teacher, Lee Kyung Ran, who changed my life. Before I met her I was always very quiet and pessimistic. I was quite a sad boy, taunted and teased because of my crippled condition. Miss Lee seemed to understand me and loved me. Probably I can say that she was the first person outside my family who gave me a great, great love. Whenever she needed something done in the classroom, she asked me to assist her. Of course I had no ability, but she guided me and showed me how to do things.

At that time my father was pastoring in a rural area and I was studying in Mokp'o. My eldest brother, my elder brother, my sister, and I were staying together. My sister was cooking for us. I was away from my parents and very,

very lonely. Miss Lee was like a mother. She spent extra time with me, teaching me how to study. She taught me how to express myself and be optimistic and how to have a singing heart.

Always I could not forget Teacher Lee. She helped me so much. She was a beautiful Christian. I cannot remember if she told me about God, but she showed Him through her love for me and her care. Through middle school, high school, and college I was thinking about her. I told myself, "When I marry and succeed in life, I will find her."

Now, it was 1988. Grace, our little daughter, Hei Jean, and I were in Baguio, Philippines. I was an ordained minister and beginning my doctoral studies at Philippine Baptist Theological Seminary. It had been nearly 20 years since I had been in Miss Lee's class. The thought came to me, "Why not try to get in touch with her? Teacher Lee would be interested in what my life is like now." I wrote a letter to the principal of San Jung School to try and locate Miss Lee. When the principal received my letter, he was deeply moved. He started a search for her. She had quit teaching about 16 years before. The principal searched for about two months. Finally, he learned that she was in Seoul and sent my letter to her. I received this letter from Teacher Lee.

October 24, 1988
My beloved student, Sung Kap:

I am so very proud of you. In Korea, all the leaves are falling now. It is autumn. My heart is really abundant, just like the farmers when they harvest. I am overwhelmed. Right now I am listening to the sound of the Olympics because my house is not far from Olympic City. I can hear celebration and shouts. Now, they are finishing a contest for the handicapped.

Now I am thinking of you. I don't know how to express my heart. Eighteen years ago I became a teacher, and my first year of teaching was at San Jung School. All of you were my beloved students. To think you have not forgotten me! I also have not forgotten you. You were a beloved student. Very often I have been thinking of all of you, wondering about whether you are married, about your children, and how I can get in touch with you. And today I received your letter. It brought back so many memories of all of you. You, Sung Kap, were handicapped. But I still remember your smile, your clear eyes, and your handsome face. It is now just as if I am looking at your face. You are so far from me; however, even though you are in a foreign country, you did not forget me. And I am so much grateful, Sung Kap.

You probably want to know about my life. I am just an ordinary person. I'm a housewife. I'm the mother of one boy and one girl. My eldest daughter is in grade three in middle school. My boy is in middle school, grade one. I am happy being a housewife. Now, you are a father and you became a minister. But I am writing to you just like you are my pupil years ago.

We are so happy and overwhelmed because of those memories. Before I started to write this letter, I had so many things to share with you, but I won't continue writing now. But let's write again. I am so grateful to the principal of San Jung Elementary School for sending me your letter. Sung Kap, please be happy and concentrate on what you are supposed to do. And in regard to your wife who I have not seen, please give her my overwhelming, happy heart. And may God bless you, my pupil Sung Kap.
Your Teacher Lee

From this letter we were continually writing to each other. When I visited my country last April, I met her at last in Seoul, after 20 years. She was living just 10 minutes away from my eldest brother's church. I remember the moment I met her at her home. She cried and embraced me. It was really a great moment. When I went down to my father's church at Mokp'o, Teacher Lee accompanied me. She attended the service when I preached. I told about her and she cried throughout the service. When we were riding the bus back to Seoul, she said, "When you were preaching you had the same smile you had 20 years ago, the very same." I stayed at her house in Seoul. Her husband was very kind to me and proud of his wife and me.

Now I must share with you, Mom, a tragedy. Teacher Lee lost her first love of the Lord Jesus Christ. She was a beautiful Christian before, but when I met her in Seoul I realized she had backslid. Her faith became like an accessory in her life. "I would like to recover that first love in my life, but I lost it," she told me. "I lost my enthusiasm to serve the Lord and my faith is not real. I've been going to church just once a week. It makes me feel better, so I go. My husband doesn't go anymore. Please pray for me, Sung Kap. When I was a Christian, I was active. I witnessed. I evangelized." Her children told her that God had sent her pupil to help her. They are active in the church. They want me to pray for all of them. So I am doing that now. I am praying that Teacher Lee will again become the full-of-joy Christian she once was.

I thought about Teacher Lee and how she lost her first love. She taught me a lesson about how important it is to keep the quiet time with our Lord. She did not keep it, and I must confess, Mom, I have not always kept it. I wrote about that:

Quiet Time

O Lord
It happened again today
Without the Word of God
Without prayer except
Three times before meals.

Throughout a week
When I opened my eyes in the morning
Instead of holding Father's hands
I lived according to my wish

Selfish living method
I proclaim the Word of God
Without a shameful reflection
That the grace of God
Poured out on His sheep
When they turned from their wicked way
But I did not think of the reality
That I might be excluded
After being used by God.

I know my main battles are not
Against flesh and blood
But not entering my heart
Not giving my time
For devotions day by day
Instead I was condemning people
Living in the Word of God
You are Old Testament Pharisees
O Lord
I do repent this ignorance.
Father allow me a quiet time with you
Which will overcome Satan's attempts
I must not live by my self-desire.

O Lord
I cannot survive even one moment
Without sharing with you
And apart from the Word of God
I lift up my life
Accept Lord my commitment
I seek to be a man of God
With my whole heart
My Father.

4

KOREA NAZARENE
THEOLOGICAL COLLEGE

(Observations from the Author)

"On yung ha say yo" was the daily greeting I received when students met me at Korea Nazarene Theological College. That is, except for Stephen. "How's it goin', Ma'am?" was his. His smile and questioning look made me feel that he really was interested in knowing how "it was goin'" with me. That infectious smile and interest continued in the classroom. He was always happy when I called on him to recite, and he always prefaced his response with "Thank you, Ma'am!"

Stephen took these chances to respond in class as opportunities to practice his English. Mastering English was both his challenge and his dream. On the bus one afternoon I asked him, "How are you?" His quick response was, "I just live one day at a time." That was one of the expressions we had discussed only a couple of hours before. Stephen enrolled in my TOEFL (Teaching of English as a Foreign Language) class when he was a sophomore. It is an advanced course in English primarily for those who plan to further their studies in Western universities. He hoped he would have this opportunity when he graduated from KNTC. He did very well in that class, as well as in others, and was recognized for having the highest grade point average in his class.

In addition to his academic excellence, Stephen did well in oratory, music, and art. I marveled at the way he turned a poem he asked me to write for KNTC Festival Days into a work of art through calligraphy and eye-catching designs. A gifted artist, he took pride in his oil paintings of still lifes and landscapes.

Editing the campus paper and organizing and leading the Holy Group were two of Stephen's other extracurricular activities at KNTC. Rev. Tim Mercer, missionary and professor of theology there, tells about Stephen's interest in forming the Holy Group: "Of special interest to me," he says, "was the way some of the students would gather around following a class lecture to probe and ask questions about entire sanctification and the life of holiness. Stephen was one of those who showed special interest beyond the formal class time. His desire to be a holy Christian and to be more aware of holiness theology led him to form the Holy Group. He took the leadership responsibility by the horns and soon the group became a very important and popular club on campus."

The campus paper was another channel by which Stephen could further the doctrine of holiness. The paper was mailed to all of the Korean Nazarene pastors. "Steve took his responsibility seriously and provided holiness sermons and Nazarene news through this medium—all in the Korean language," wrote Dr. Kenneth Pearsall, interim president of KNTC during the academic year 1983-84. "When I wrote a sermon in English, Stephen translated it into the Korean language so the local pastors would have some resource materials. Knowing the lack of holiness literature in his native language, Stephen went to great lengths to supply the need."

He met some of my needs too. Through our association beyond the classroom, as well as in it, Stephen became a caring, helpful friend. At times he sensed my frustration over not being able to speak or understand Korean. In chapel one day while the student body president was preaching, a note found its way along a pew to me: "He is preaching about righteousness," it read. "Can you understand? Maybe. Stephen."

My TOEFL class was at night. When it was over, Bill Patch, the president of KNTC, would take me to the bus station. There I would take the bus to Taejon, an hour's ride. One evening I missed the last bus going to Taejon, where I lived. "What do I do now?" I wondered aloud. Stephen had a ready answer, "You can take the train, Ma'am." I hadn't been on a Korean train before nor in a Korean train station. I didn't know where the Ch'onan City train station was or those in Taejon.

Stephen came to my rescue. "I will help you, Ma'am," he said. He had a taxi take us to the train station. He bought my ticket, waited 40 minutes with me, and wrote directions for the taxi driver in Taejon to take me to my house. When the train arrived, he limped on it with me, pushed me through several coaches to my seat, and gave instructions to the people sitting behind me to let me know when we reached Taejon and the right station. He barely had enough time to limp off into the cold before the train began moving. The carnation and I weathered the trip well. The carnation was a gift from Stephen.

Stephen helped me in other ways. He seemed to think it was both a privilege and a duty to inform me about Korean customs and food. I welcomed the information. On the ferry to Cheju Island, KNTC students and I had a late supper of soup and kimchi. Stephen said, "Ma'am, I will tell you how the soup is made. In water, a cow's head is put . . ." Rice, slivers of meat, onions, and lots of broth were the ingredients, along with an egg yolk floating on top. Apparently, it was added just before the soup was brought from the kitchen. Stirring the soup first, as everyone did, made the soup yellow. Since I had had three eggs already that day, I put my yolk in Stephen's bowl.

On another occasion I asked Stephen about a white, slippery-looking food. "Acupunc-?" he asked.

"No," I said, "it can't be *that!* Do you mean 'octopus'?"

"Yes," he said, happy to learn another English word.

Stephen was as interested in food as I was. I always enjoyed the artistry displayed in the dishes; Stephen enjoyed eating them. Kimchi was his favorite, as it is of most Koreans. Made from Chinese cabbage, onions, garlic, red peppers, and spices, it is stored in earthen jars and lasts for several months. Koreans eat it three times a day. Stephen would have liked to eat it more often!

I felt that I knew Stephen much better after I visited his father's church and family in Mokp'o, on the southern coast of the Korean peninsula. After the Sunday morning service, he took me up to the flat roof. A beautiful panorama met our eyes—acres of roofs, mountains behind us, and before us the Yellow Sea stretching to the horizon. Stephen talked about his father's pioneer work in the rural area for the Church of the Nazarene, about the church we were in, and another in Mokp'o that his father's church had organized. He also talked about his own hopes and dreams, and with tears in his eyes, his desire to enter the ministry.

Stephen and Grace began dating when they were sophomores at KNTC. Although she was in one of my literature classes at that time, I did not really become acquainted with Grace until later after she had lost some of her shyness. When Stephen mentioned her name one afternoon, I told him, "Miss Ihm is pretty." They were going steady as far as I knew. His face brightened; then a shadow spread over it.

"Thank you, Ma'am," he said. "Her father does not like me." When I questioned him about the reason, he said, "Because of my body." Stephen's childhood polio had indeed left him crippled. But I seldom was aware of that, for his zest for life and learning, his participation in nearly every area of campus life, and his continual optimism superseded his physical handicap. When he led the singing in children's meetings, he stepped freely about with his guitar or tambourine, his crippled leg seeming not to hinder his graceful movements. At KNTC picnics he was asked to take his guitar and lead the singing. It was impossible for him to stand still.

So I was surprised when he told me that Grace's father did not like him. In a way, however, I was not too surprised, for I knew from my reading that many Koreans look upon physical handicaps as serious obstacles to marriage and certain professions. The Ministry of Education, for instance, set up controversial guidelines concerning those whom teachers' colleges should not admit. They included people who "cannot pass the public officials' physical test regulations, who have features causing displeasure to others," and a number of other regulations.

Stephen told me that his father and Grace's would soon be meeting to talk about further plans for him and Grace. The conference ended happily and before long I received an invitation to Grace's home for a celebration announcing their engagement.

Rather than a party, it was more like a church service but around festive tables. Little dishes of crisp seaweed squares, white squid, rice cakes, and other special dishes were on tables in three little rooms. In one room were the wives of the missionaries, Stephen's elder brother (Koreans don't use given names nearly so much as "eldest brother," "elder brother," "youngest sister," etc., when they refer to members of their families), his sister, father, mother, and me. In another room were the male missionaries, who were also professors at KNTC, District Superintendent Oh, Stephen, and Grace in a pretty pink *hanbok,* the traditional dress of Koreans. Several KNTC students ate in a third room. Grace's mother stayed busy in the kitchen but donned a pink *hanbok* for picture-taking. A hymn, prayers, a sermonette by Rev. Oh, the exchange of rings, were all parts of the engagement ceremony. This, I was told, was nearly as binding as a wedding ceremony.

That was September 13, 1982. In May the next year, I attended Stephen's and Grace's wedding in the Nazarene church where Stephen was associate pastor. Grace stood with downcast eyes throughout the hour-long service. If she smiled, she would give birth to only girls Stephen told me when I commented on her seriousness throughout the wedding. (She must have smiled sometime during the service, for the Kims' first child was a girl!)

I accompanied Stephen and Grace on their honeymoon. The entire senior class did also. That was the latter part of May. Stephen and Grace waited until then to go on their honeymoon, for the senior trip was to the place they and all Korean honeymooners dream of going—Cheju Island. It's the largest and most famous of the islands off the southern coast of the Korean peninsula. A six-hour ferry ride from the mainland, this "Garden of the Gods," as it is called, has all that anyone could wish for: Mount Halla, the highest mountain in Korea, with a crater lake at its summit; cascading waterfalls; Dragon Rock emerging from the sea and raising its angry black head high in the air; some of the longest caves in the world; fragrant orange groves; a storm-polished driftwood park; daring women

Senior Class on Cheju Island; Stephen and Grace, fourth and fifth from right

deep-sea diving in churning waters for shellfish. Add to these a history of enchanting legends and quiet beauty and you have a province of Korea that not only Koreans, but people throughout the world, dream of visiting.

During our six-hour train trip from Ch'onan City to Mokp'o, where we would visit Stephen's home and board the ferry, Stephen and Grace were our host and hostess. Stephen's mother had lunch ready when we arrived at the parsonage in the Bethel Church of the Nazarene. His father was not at home. Stephen again acted as host and placed Rev. Kang, KNTC's chaplain and senior class sponsor, and me at a little table in a room by ourselves. Mrs. Kim, attractive and self-effacing, served us seaweed soup and special dishes, including octopus and clams in shells. When we finished eating, Stephen and his classmates made short work of what remained. We then boarded the ferry for our trip to Cheju Island.

Most of the students climbed Mount Halla, a feat that every other Korean who steps foot on Cheju-do thinks he must accomplish. Stephen, Grace, Miss Kim, her son, and I awaited their return in a lovely vale surrounded by mountains. I learned that this special part of the park was a courtesy offered us by the manager. Stephen had told him, "She is a professor."

We five became quite well-acquainted during the six hours the others were climbing Mount Halla. For a while we walked up the trail toward the summit, spent some time in a lava rock-filled ravine, and listened to the music of the birds there. I enjoyed watching Stephen thread his way around some boulders and over others, meeting the challenge they presented to his crippled leg. Boxes of *kimbop*, little rounds of pressed rice, were our lunch. I was glad to have Stephen nearby to finish mine.

We left the island on an evening flight to Seoul and then took a train to Ch'onan City. I was the only one to go on to Taejon. My reserved seat was only to Ch'onan. Stephen wanted to make sure that I would not have to stand the rest of the trip, so he talked with several attendants about finding me a seat. He must have succeeded in convincing someone that "My professor must sit." Much to my embarrassment, an attendant ordered a fellow to get up and give me his seat.

That time with Korean students was the highlight of my two years in Korea. That was partly because of Stephen and Grace. They and the others had been my teachers, I, the learner. Through their warmth, concern, and sensitivity, they showed by example rather than by words the Christian Way.

5

ASIA-PACIFIC NAZARENE THEOLOGICAL SEMINARY

Stephen and Grace began a new life in April 1984 when they moved to the Philippines to study at Asia-Pacific Nazarene Theological Seminary in Manila. Grace talks about that time:

When we arrived in the Philippines, three Nazarene missionaries met us—Mrs. Adeline Owens, Pamela Grant, and Eunice Marlin. Pamela and Eunice were working in the regional office. Now Pamela is in Haiti and Eunice is teaching at Luzon Nazarene Bible College in Baguio. They took us to the regional office in Manila. There Mrs. Owens prayed for us. Her prayer was full of tears as she committed us to the Lord. How well we remember that time!

I remember, too, those first few days in the Philippines. Dr. and Mrs. Owens (Dr. Owens was the president of APNTS then) took us around Manila and introduced us to the shopping center. They took care of us and even bought things for us. We'll never forget their great concern. Indeed, they are our spiritual parents.

Stephen shows his excitement in a letter about their new life:

May 22, 1984
Dear My special Ma'am:

Hallelujah! Greetings in Jesus' name who saved us from our sins. Praise the Lord! Always our Lord Jesus

Christ gives new living water to my heart.

How delighted we were to receive your letter when we arrived in Manila from Korea. We received it from Mrs. Kyle Greene, who is a missionary. It was really good to begin our new life in the Philippines with your letter. Thank you very much for sending it. I am sorry my reply letter is late.

You know, Ma'am, here it is very hot weather during the whole year. It was difficult for us to adjust. But nowadays we are very fine in many ways because of many people's kindly guidance, concern, and prayers.

Grace and I attended the first summer session at APNTS as soon as we arrived here. Now we are very busy preparing for the second summer session and for the regular semester classes. I will study for a master of divinity degree and Grace for a masters in religious education. I think our main problem will be reading and writing in English rather than in speaking English. I trust that if we study continually day by day, this problem will be solved one day.

There are several reasons why we decided to study in the Philippines. The first is that I have a big concern for missions in Asia. God gave me a vision about this when I experienced salvation in Christ. Another reason is to increase my English ability. I came also because of our economic problem. After finishing my degree here, I hope that I can enter a doctoral program in America . . . After our preparation we will go back to Korea.

Grace and I are living in a family apartment on our campus. Our seminary gives us all of the necessities of life so we can cook and Grace can make many kinds of kimchi for me. I am a kimchi killer still! . . . Every morning we have early morning prayer meeting together at my home. We read the Bible, give testimonies, sing and pray loudly. Especially, I pray for Ma'am's health and your continual efforts for God's kingdom. Grace is praying for you too.

Really, Grace and I are missing you so much. We put your picture on the desk so we can see you every time. Some people here know you very well and some know

about me through the *World Mission* magazine from Rev. Stults that you sent to him for me. That was very special to me. One professor put it on the notice board in a seminary building. The article is a wonderful grace that God can use in His ministry. We do not forget that God leads our lives. We pray that we will live for only our Lord Jesus Christ, our Savior. We have thankful minds that we met you and that you have special concerns for us . . .
God's richest blessings on you.
Sincerely,
Stephen Kim

Dr. Kenneth Pearsall attended the APNTS dedication the next year. "I found both Stephen and Grace," he said, "continuing their leadership roles. They had started early morning prayer meetings for the Korean students and any other students who wanted to attend. They were active in local Nazarene churches. Yes, they were homesick for Korean food and friends, but they refused to be despondent. They were overcomers through their faith."

Among Stephen's other extracurricular activities were editing the APNTS campus newsletter and heading up an important seminary ministry in Tondo, an inner-city slum area. (The latter is treated in a separate chapter.)

Generally, all was going well with the Kims. Stephen enjoyed campus life and also his experiences in becoming acquainted with Manila. He and Grace were enjoying life on the campus, their studies, and their ministry. They knew now what God had in mind for their future. In one of his letters Stephen wrote: "Last year was the most significant year for both of us. God showed us the right way that we ought to go. We do praise the Lord that He purifies our motives for studying. The Holy Spirit gives us wisdom to dedicate ourselves wholly. God is calling us to a special pastoral ministry for the handicapped in Korea, along with a publications ministry. The publications ministry will relate to them. There are millions of physically impaired people in Korea who don't know who Jesus Christ is yet. Grace and I are willing to obey God's will in being instruments to deliver the message of entire sanctification."

The Kims were also thrilled that their first child was due in a few months. They were happy to share the news with Stephen's mother:

Before Grace and I had our first baby, I called my mother in Korea and said, "Mom, Grace is pregnant."

Her first words were, "Oh, Son, I know it will be a boy!"

"No, Mom, it will be a girl," I told her.

"How do you know that?" she asked.

I said, "Probably because of Grace's face and its beautiful color. People say it will be a girl."

"Son, please have deep faith and pray, pray that it will be a boy!" my mother said.

When Grace delivered a girl and I called my mother, I told her, "Mom, I told you it would be a girl."

She said, "OK, it doesn't matter. Don't be discouraged. But I'm sure next time God will give you a boy." She was encouraging us to have another baby.

So when Grace was pregnant again, my mother prayed for a boy. We were praying, too, for a boy. We were preparing everything with a blue color. The first time we were preparing everything with a pink color. I don't know why we knew our first baby would be a girl. My mother and we were very, very happy when Grace delivered a boy.

I must tell you, Mom, why we named our little girl "Hei Jean." Since the time Grace became pregnant, we started 1,000 prayers, praying for true wisdom for our child. Like Solomon, we prayed for wisdom. We had prayed about 650 times when Grace delivered. We named our baby "Hei Jean." "Hei" means "wisdom," "Jean" means "true"—"True Wisdom." We continued our prayers about needing wisdom to guide Hei Jean so that she would as early as possible accept our Lord Jesus Christ.

A Christian doctor delivered Hei Jean. From the first checkup to the last when she delivered Hei Jean, she did not charge us a single centavo. She said, "Pastor, I did it for the Lord." We paid for only the hospital expenses. The doctor is still a good friend of ours.

Unfortunately, another pediatrician gave Hei Jean some wrong medicine. Three days after she was born, she had to be hospitalized for a week. At that time we didn't have any money. We prayed, "O Lord, please provide for our expenses." When our baby was discharged from the hospital, the medical expenses were 8,200 pesos, over $400. Do you know what happened, Mom? God sent us 8,200 pesos exactly. This came from a friend in the United States.

We watched Hei Jean grow and praised the Lord for her. Grace wrote a poem about her that we would like to share with you.

Hei Jean, My Precious One

Day by day I store
My prayers deep in my heart
The secret of joy flows
Through me
And it reaches to heaven.

You are the constant benefit
Of God to me
You are in my arms
You are His one
Who loves a single soul
More than a universe.

Oh! my darling
I can do nothing for you
But I do not have fear
There's only overbrimming joy
Through you
And thanksgiving to God
In Thy wonderful love
In Thy righteous will.

The way you ought to go
Is a narrow road
But remember my lovely daughter
Always the invisible hands of God
Shall hold your hands.

Keep your pure image
Before the Lord
Keep your humble heart
Before the Lord
Keep never changing faith
Before the Lord.

Do your best to present
Your entire self to Him
As one approved.

I pray with
Tears of joy for you
Follow the footprints
Of Jesus Christ who sent you
Love your neighbors
Seek first the kingdom of God
And His righteousness
Thus you can let them know
The love of God
Through your living sacrifice.

My beloved daughter
My precious child
Write the Word of truth
Indelibly on your heart.

You are in my arms
As a beautiful image
You are also His forever.

Stephen, Grace, and Hei Jean were a happy, hopeful family. Stephen's optimism is expressed in his Easter 1987 letter:

Dear Dr. Laughbaum, our Mom in the Lord:

Praise the Lord for Christ's victory over death! We don't know yet the American way of celebrating Easter, but we are learning the Filipino way—sunrise service and marching in the street.

Thank you very much for your love along with your prayers. I can tell you that it was an answer to our prayers when we received the money from you.

This is my last week of classes at APNTS. My last requirement is five pages of critique, which I have to submit by Friday. Well, God has really blessed my family during the last three years. We are sending a fan for an Easter present. It's the Korean way, I guess. Baby Hei Jean's marks are on the box. Perhaps she also wants to celebrate Easter with you . . .

We love you and are praying for you.
2 Tim. 2:15
With love and prayers,
Jean, Grace, and Stephen

The Kims were enjoying life to the fullest. Then a bomb dropped. Stephen told about it:

I became very ill. I could not eat anything. Even if I drank water, I vomited. I also had terrible headaches and double vision. Some of these were the same symptoms I had years before when I was at KNTC and fasted and prayed. Now, seven years later it was happening again.

The doctors said I needed brain surgery. I knew that would be an extremely serious operation and that I might not live. However, I was not afraid. I had the conviction that, for me, death meant that when I closed my eyes and then opened them, I would be in the arms of our Lord Jesus Christ. I shared this view with others when they asked me, "What does death mean to you?"

Probably, I was almost dead when I was taken to the hospital. I don't know how I survived because for a long time I could not eat and those terrible headaches and double vision continued. When the doctors at the hospital examined me, they found a tumor on my brain.

For about two weeks before the operation, I was being prepared for it through IVs, etc. For the first operation they put a tube behind my ear, past my neck, and connected it to my brain. Even now, this tube is taking down water from the brain to the bladder. This was the first operation. The second one took about 12 hours. They removed two tumors.

I experienced a great, great love at this time through my friends and especially the missionaries, who surrounded me. When I was in the hospital, Mrs. Fairbanks, wife of the APNTS president at that time, came and shared with me one morning. She said, "Last night when I had my devotions, I asked the Lord, 'Why is Stephen suffering like this?'" God showed her a scripture related to some purposes of suffering, that through it one learns more about obeying God's will and experiencing His lovingkindness. Through this experience God told her, "Stephen will learn there is something I want to do through him. It is not because of any sin of his or of his parents, but for the sake of My will. I am going to do something for Stephen because of this experience."

Anne Fairbanks really impressed me with her love. She was the spiritual mother on the APNTS campus.

Mildred Gibson, Neva Beech, and Jo Edlin always came to the hospital and asked Grace what she needed. "Do you need disposable diapers?" they asked. "What would you like to eat?" Always they were bringing, one by one, everything we needed. They even made a schedule for staying with Grace. She was never alone. They scheduled friends and students to be at the hospital with me. I heard that Dr. Edlin had all of the students meet in the chapel at midnight to pray for me. Through their prayers God healed me.

I must mention about the sacrificial love of Jo Edlin. I will never forget it. She was the campus nurse at that time. She became a very, very special friend of ours. She was the one who, after my first operation, took care of me throughout my physical struggles.

Between my brain surgeries while I was waiting at home for the second one, two Korean women visited us. They said, "Brother, we were praying for you last night and God revealed to us that you need to repent. If you don't repent, even though you have a second operation, you may be dead. It's because of your sin you are this way. You must repent." I was struggling a lot. Just like Job's friends, I thought. But I just said, "Thank you for your prayers."

My mother was with me at that time. She said, "I cannot understand how they can say that." What these women said to me almost killed me again.

After about four months one of the women came to me and asked my forgiveness. "Brother Kim," she said, "I am very sorry. It was my spiritual pride. Will you forgive me?" I did. The other woman left for Korea without ever asking my forgiveness.

After my first operation I prayed for myself and had such a conviction that God would heal me so that I would not need a second operation. I told Dr. Fairbanks, "God will hear my prayer. He will heal me."

Dr. Fairbanks said, "Stephen, I understand how you feel. You are burdened about the medical expenses. But, you see, we Nazarenes and the church around the world are praying for you, and we are willing to help you. Please submit yourself to this operation. Without it, you will not be able to survive."

But I kept telling him, "No, I think God will heal me. I think He has already healed me, so I won't need another operation." The doctors told me if I thought this was the case, I should have another physical examination. I agreed.

Dr. Edlin took me to a Chinese hospital two and a half hours from the seminary for the examination. While we were going there, I had a vision. The vision was two pieces of blood came out of the back of my head. They were about the size of my hand. The vision was very clear.

I said to Dr. Edlin, "I saw a vision. Two pieces of blood came out of my head."

He responded, "How much I wish that were true, Stephen."

At the hospital the doctor told me, "I think the examination is useless, for I know the tumor is still there."

But I insisted, "No, it's already gone. God healed me." I still had the conviction that God healed me.

I had the examination. Two doctors showed me the X rays and gave an explanation. "Mr. Kim," they said, "look at these pictures." There were many of them. "Can you see this first picture? The tumor is clear. Can you see this one? It's clear the tumor is still there. There it is, your tumor. Now look on the other side. The same thing. What do you say now?"

By this time, Mom, I was crying. "What about the vision?" I asked myself. It came to me later that perhaps it was a picture of what took place during the operation.

After the surgery I had a terrible pain in my right foot. The doctors said it was because of polio I had many years ago. The pain was like someone was piercing my foot with a nail or sword. It was so bad that I didn't know how to deal with it. I used a pain injection for nine months. Doctors told me that I must be very careful about using it, for I could become addicted. But I had to have it. I don't think I could have survived without it.

One day Grace was out, and I was alone at home. I called Jo Edlin for an injection. Sue Stults was with her. She smiled and said, "I came along for moral support." That was strange. I could not understand what she was talking about. I thought, There is nothing moral or immoral about just having an injection in my arm. Not even in my hip. Why were they talking about *moral* support? I learned this has a different meaning in America than it does in Korea.

Because of the pain in my foot, I had to visit several other doctors, leg and foot specialists. One advised me to take an electric shock treatment. He put an injection in my backbone and leg and connected some kind of electrical instrument. It took about six hours for sending all of the electric shocks. There were about six sheets of computer research to find the source of my pain.

The next day the doctor told me, "We have found the source of your pain. It comes from your back."

I asked him, "How are you going to solve this problem?"

He said, "Now that we have found the cause and where the pain comes from, we can treat you."

However, they could not solve my problem. I suffered continually because of the pain, but they did not help me. I decided to see an acupuncturist, Mr. Kim. He was a Korean to whom I was referred by one of my Korean friends. He touched my hand and my body and then he said, "Your pain is coming from your back above the hip." I laughed. I told him, "I had electric shocks for about six hours to find the pain and now you are telling me this just by touching me!"

He was the one who stopped the pain injections. After two months I didn't use it anymore. I was so grateful.

Grace told about the time of Stephen's critical illness:

Every day I prayed with tears, "O Lord, please raise Stephen up again. I am committing him to You, leaving everything in Your hands. But please let Stephen live."

Who knows how many tears I shed? That was the most difficult time for me in this foreign country. But I was never alone. God sent me so many prayer supporters. They were closer to me and more sincere than my own family and relatives. They are our spiritual brothers and sisters and really took care of us. They loved us and helped us financially.

So many people surrounded us, especially the Fairbankses and the Edlins. They are our prayer partners, and I shall never forget their love. I thank God for the great leadership of these scholars and professors. Now, Dr. Fairbanks is the president of Mount Vernon Nazarene College and Dr. Edlin is a professor at MidAmerica Nazarene College.

Because of the wonderful Christian life of the missionaries, I learned many things. They showed us what the real Christian life is. From Anne Fairbanks I learned many things about being a pastor's wife. Whenever I had difficult times, she showed me how to deal with the challenges and trials. Every day when she came to the hospital she shared a message with us from her personal devotions. So many times Anne was alone on the campus when Dr. Fairbanks was traveling on business and promotion trips for the seminary. Yet she was always sharing with me as a spiritual mother. That was really a great, great encouragement to me.

It was by the grace of God that I was able to meet Mrs. Jo Edlin. I can say she is a born nurse, just like my elder sister. Do you know, Mom, when Stephen was in the hospital and I was sad and crying, she cried with me. When I was really depressed and discouraged, she embraced my hurting and broken heart. When Stephen had his operations, Jo Edlin was with me. She knew about my lack of English and so she was the one who met the doctors. Through all of the procedures and tests, she was with me. At that time I thought that Jo and Jim Edlin were doing things only for my family. But after they left APNTS we heard from so many others for whom they did the same things. That love, that care, that concern, those tears, testify to a beautiful Christian life. I learned from them.

After Stephen's first operation, Sandi Patti was here for a concert. Jo was with seminary students at the concert. The next day she brought several of Sandi Patti's tapes to the hospital. She could not use the electricity there, so she bought batteries. She said she was thinking of me all through the concert, from the first song to the last. The messages of the songs were just as if they had been meant for me. Indeed, Jo is my eldest sister.

God provided us with good doctors and even provided all of our medical expenses through Nazarene worldwide participation in special offerings. Through so much love, concern, and prayers, God raised Stephen up. I say, "Hallelujah!" We are debtors of the love of Jesus Christ, and now is the time to share this love. Always we have received, now we must return it to others. . . .

In planning for the future of APNTS, Dr. Fairbanks and Dr. Edlin, academic dean, wanted to expand the number of Asian and South Pacific faculty members as quickly as possible. They saw in Stephen the potential "for a long-term relationship with APNTS as a faculty member." Following his release from the hospital and graduation from the seminary, Stephen was encouraged to consider the master of theology degree program in biblical studies offered in Manila through the Asia Graduate School of Theology. He applied for the program and was accepted but missed his first module because of illness. After his long period of recovery, he enrolled in a doctoral program at Philippine Baptist Theological Seminary in Baguio. "We were beginning to discuss the possibility of a teaching internship at APNTS," Dr. Fairbanks said, "following Stephen's completion of his course work for the program."

6

INNER-CITY MINISTRY IN MANILA

Stephen's ministry in Tondo, an inner-city area in Manila, began in 1984, not long after he enrolled at APNTS. He was a volunteer worker at that time. Through contacts Stephen made in the Tondo District, especially related to the mission efforts of a Korean church there, APNTS began a ministry in the area. A part of it was assisting in a medical clinic, situated in a landfill area near the Manila North Harbor. Believers provided two rooms for the clinic. A letter from Stephen tells about his Tondo ministry:

Dear Dr. Laughbaum:

The Oriental Medical Mission Association appointed me as a Korean missionary in the slum area of Tondo last April 1987. I do believe that God sent me here in the Philippines not only for study but also for preparation for the ministry. I must be disciplined for compassionate ministry as well as for publication ministry.

Approximately 30 people, including American professors from APNTS, are participating in our medical mission in Tondo, an inner-city slum area. The 2 million people here are extremely poor. When they accept Jesus Christ as Lord and Savior, they are very active. God has performed many miracles here. I am really happy to be serving these Asians.

Please pray for this special ministry. Sometimes it is dangerous work, both because of the slum area and the New People's Army (Communists). Two church people [an independent church] were killed by the NPA January 6, 1988. I was not there at that time, but my Korean friend was leading the worship service and two NPA's appeared just to shoot. I used to go there and am working in that area. We need prayers, too, because of the liquor and drugs in this place . . .

I will share with you some more stories next time. Good-bye.

Stephen, Your very close friend

Stephen tells about the time he first began ministering in Tondo, as well as his later work there:

When I would mention ministering in Tondo, people were surprised and warned me. So many people warned me. They said, "That is a slum area and a very dangerous place, a notorious place."

Several years ago when a criminal was running away and police were trying to catch him, if he passed a certain bridge to enter Tondo, the police had to stop right there. For if they crossed the bridge, they would be killed by other criminals. So even the police were afraid to enter this area until the pope came. He visited Tondo, kissed the ground, and the situation has been better since that time.

When I talked about my work to my friends at APNTS, I told them, "I know where Tondo is, what it is, and how to travel there."

They asked me, "Why are you ministering *there?* Why are you risking your life? Why? You should not work *there.* They're dangerous, they're criminals, you may be killed."

I asked them, "Have you been there?" They had not been there, yet they were warning me.

You know, Mom, people in Tondo, they are really wonderful people. When they knew I was sacrificing my life there, they really helped and encouraged me. They are beautiful people, very simple. When they realize you want to evangelize, they love you with an unusual love. I have experienced this love in my Tondo ministry.

I helped organize a workshop, called on participants, and trained them to help in a medical clinic. We had to find doctors and dentists and nurses to assist them. They were a missionary dentist, Choi Chang Whan from Korea; another dentist, Dr. Jerome Villalon, a Nazarene; and two Nazarene doctors, Marietta Villalon and Vivan Edrozo. They would recommend medicines, and I bought them in Manila. Always I negotiated the price in order to buy more medicines. I was in this medical mission for three years, even after my brain surgeries when I was on crutches.

I will tell you, Mom, how we did this work. We had eight tables. The first table was the Entrance Table. Here we prepared treatment forms the people must fill out; name, age, sex, religion, address. Table No. 2 was the Doctors' Table. Two or three nurses were there to take blood pressure and temperature. The doctors examined the patients and then prescribed.

[Ronald Beech, APNTS faculty member, was at Table No. 3, the Vitamin Table. "I was assigned to the Vitamin Table again this time," he said. "I suppose the feeling was that a seminary faculty member could at least count out a 30-day supply of vitamins and tie them securely in a little plastic bag!" ("Unto the Least of These . . . ," *World Mission*, December 1988.)]

Table No. 4 was the Cough and Cold section. Because of typhoons and rainy seasons and in the nighttime the people did not have blankets, they caught many colds. In this section we had cough syrup, serums and tablets, and drops for the children. We instructed the people how to give them and about the dosages.

Table 5 was the Worming section. You know, Mom, in this area the people were living on garbage. They did not even have shoes, so they got so many worms. Garbage was widely spread in some parts of Tondo. That's why when we entered Tondo, a garbage smell was very strong there. When they collected this garbage about five years ago, they received only five pesos, which is about 50 cents.

Table 6 was the Diarrhea section. When the people had money, they used it for food. They could not use it for fuel for fire to boil water. Not boiling the water caused diarrhea.

Table 7 was the Skin Disease section. We applied antibiotic cream, which was very, very expensive.

Table 8 was the Specific Diseases section, like high and low blood pressure, asthma, and typhoid. Especially with typhoid, they had to have a doctor's prescription before they could have medicine.

At all of these tables before we gave medicine or treatments, we laid our hands on the patients and prayed

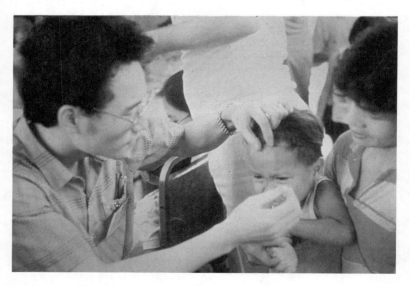

Clinic work in Tondo

for them. We prayed with tears for them, and they were deeply moved by the prayers and sacrifice of our people.

I mentioned, Mom, that I experienced several miracles in my Tondo ministry. I'll share one of them. When we saw one woman at the medical mission, the left side of her stomach was swollen. She asked us for medicine. She said because of extreme undernourishment she had even been worse two months earlier, but she had no money for follow-up medication. The doctors examined her and said if she didn't have surgery immediately, she would die.

But there was no money. I called all of the young people together. I had a little money, enough for some McDonald's hamburgers for our workers. That was 500 pesos; five years ago that was about $25.00. I explained the situation to them and asked, "What shall we do?" They all agreed they would fast and we would give the money for the woman's operation.

So we took her to Tondo General Hospital. Do you know how much that operation and her expenses were? Exactly 500 pesos! This hospital doesn't charge much. In Manila it would have been about 4,000 pesos. Through that operation she was completely healed. When we had the next medical clinic, she was there. I did not recognize her face, for she was very beautiful. She cried and cried and held my hand. She spoke in Tagalog, "Thank you, thank you, Sir." She became a very active member of our church in Tondo.

I did visitation in one of the worst areas in Tondo. It's easy to get lost there. The houses are many and very small, like our dining table. They do not have wood walls, only plastic. One time when I was doing visitation, they offered me food. It was rice and dried fish, which was very smelly, and soup. There was no spoon or fork. I had to use my fingers to put the rice in the soup and eat it with the fish. I had to do it because I really wanted to let them know that I loved them. When they saw me eating with my fingers, they told me, "Pastor, you love us." When I got home, I had diarrhea for more than a week. I never forgot that time.

God also provided me with the opportunity to work in the Tondo city jail. We had a Bible study there. Another group from a prominent sect, Iglesia Ni Cristo, had a Bible study there too. They would bring bread and distribute it during the Bible study. But we had no bread for lack of money. That group and a Catholic group [Catholicism is strong in the Philippines] joined our group for some of the sessions.

One time two young men came to the jail looking for a job. In Tondo it is very difficult to get work. It was strange they came to the jail. A worker there sent them to me, and I told them, "Let's pray about it together. We will see how the Lord will lead you." Later we hired one of the men to do janitorial work in the church. Sometime afterward two young men were released from jail. They became Christians. I called them and asked, "Would you like to return to the city jail?"

"What?" they said. "How can you talk to us like that? We're just out of jail."

"We have a Bible study there," I told them, "and we need some assistance. If you would help us, you could show the prisoners how beautiful your changed life is because you have been changed by our Lord Jesus Christ. Then you can work outside collecting garbage and earning money."

They helped us in our Bible study. When their friends came and saw their changed lives, they accepted the Lord. That was a miracle! We also had a ministry in a mental hospital in Tondo. My American friend, Philip Galley, held a Bible study there. He was my very close friend, a miracle man, and a man of God. He invited me to help him in the Bible study.

I remember very well the first time I went to the mental hospital. When I entered the second floor, the nurse locked the door from the inside. I was really scared then. I asked her, "Why do you lock the door? Why?"

"Are you afraid?" she asked.

I told her I was really scared. "What if they join together and hurt me?" I asked.

She said, "Don't you know, Pastor Kim, these mental patients, they can never unite to hurt others. They are playing against each other because of their mental problems. They will never unite. Don't worry."

Some ladies came to embrace me and asked me to listen to them. They wanted attention from us. Philip told them in his Bible study, "Today I have my friend here, Brother Stephen Kim, who is in the last year of working for his master of divinity degree. He's a scholar. Whatever you want to ask today, don't worry, because he will answer you."

Mom, I was worried! There was Philip with a Catholic Bible in one hand and a Protestant Bible in the other. He had memorized a great deal of the Bible. He knew so much about the Bible, and he was only a layperson. I was deeply impressed. The questions from these patients, oh, they were very, very difficult—high standard questions, for some of the patients were from seminaries. Now, Philip was saying, "Stephen will answer your questions." I had to tell him, "Sorry, Brother Phil, I will come next Wednesday and will answer them then. But for today give me a break." You know, Mom, as he was sharing stories from the Bible, honestly, there were several that I heard for the first time. Oh, I was really ashamed about this and embarrassed about not answering the questions.

When they saw me limping, they asked, "What happened to your leg?" "Come back next Wednesday," I told them, "and I will give you my testimony." That's what I did. I told them how I became a cripple and how by the grace of God, I was able to walk again. When I finished talking and came down from the pulpit, quickly one lady asked me the same question, "What happened to your leg?" Some of the patients were able to catch what I told them, but others were not.

That was really an experience for me because of my American friend, Brother Philip. He showed me an amazing, beautiful Christian life.

God really blessed me, Mom, in all of these ministries, and I saw many victories. But I didn't always have victory in my heart. Let me explain. First, I would like to say there are positive examples and negative examples. Everyone likes to follow a person who is talented and successful. Philip is a positive example. Mom, I am a negative example many times. I fail, I'm weak, I have a wrong attitude. Sometimes in my ministry in the Tondo slums area, I had wrong motives and attitudes, but I pray that God can use even a negative example. Perhaps people can learn from me and not follow my example.

7

PHILIPPINE BAPTIST THEOLOGICAL SEMINARY

The day that I left APNTS, Grace told me, I was with my little girl, Hei Jean. Stephen was already in Baguio. A Korean friend went with him to orientation at the seminary because he could not travel by himself. We put all our things in the car. It was raining. More than 10 Koreans were with us. We stood together and they prayed for my family. I cried during that prayer. I suddenly realized that I was about to leave my friends, move to a distant city in this foreign country, and enter an unknown life. How I wished that we were moving home to Korea! I had not seen my country since coming to the Philippines four years ago.

But Stephen had been greatly challenged to enter the doctoral program in Baguio in spite of physical problems. Many people advised him not to do it, but we knew it was the will of God. In spite of our friends' concern and advice, Stephen told them, "Thank you for your prayers and concern, but God clearly showed me what I am supposed to do."

Several weeks ago Timothy, our APNTS classmate and prayer partner, took Stephen to Baguio for the entrance examination and took care of him in the classroom. Stephen was on crutches and could not see very well because of double vision. Timothy was indeed Stephen's hands and legs.

The examination lasted from morning until evening. Stephen had to take one in English and one in theology, on eight different subjects. He said it was the most difficult examination he had ever taken. He completed it, and after several days received a letter from the seminary that he had passed and was accepted into the doctoral program.

And now I would join Stephen soon in Baguio. That was God's plan. While my friends prayed, my thoughts turned to their concern for us and to all the love and care of our friends at APNTS, and of God's love. In my heart I prayed, "Lord, now I'm leaving for Baguio. A new life and a new challenge are before me. I will do my best to obey Your will, whatever You offer me or ask me to do." I committed everything to the Lord, for He is the one who leads and shows the future . . .

I was on crutches then, Stephen said. Whenever it rained, I needed four arms. Two carrying my crutches, another for my books, another for my umbrella. When it rained (it rains a lot here) the pain in my foot was more terrible and my head ached more. My eye problem became more severe. It was very difficult to read because I could not focus my eyes. Doctoral study, you know, Mom, requires a lot of reading. I was enjoying my Old Testament classes—I was working on a degree in Old Testament theology—but Greek and Hebrew were difficult for me.

I became discouraged at times, both during my graduate work at the seminary here and later when I was a pastor in Baguio. Mom, do you know my source of encouragement during these times? Our precious children. God has shown His love to us during our years in the Philippines by giving us gifts, a daughter and a son. Hei Jean was born April 12, 1986, two years after we came to Manila. Paul was born May 28, 1990, in Baguio.

Hei Jean will soon be five. She is a product of the Philippines. However, she is fluent in both Korean and English. We are praying that perhaps someday she will serve our Lord through a ministry in music. Hei Jean is a girl of prayer. She was a real encouragement to me when I had difficulty dealing with my pain. When I was in the dormitory at the seminary, I was groaning and said, "I have pain."

Hei Jean said, "I will come to you." She would lay her hands on my foot and pray, with tears, "Jesus, please heal Daddy's pain." After her prayer she always asked me, "How about now?"

I had to answer her, "Oh, now everything's gone! Now it's fine." She was very happy. But I had the same pain. When she heard me groaning again, she complained, "Daddy, I prayed for you. Why are you still sick?" I had to tell Grace to leave with her.

When I went up or down stairs, Hei Jean always came to hold my hand. "Daddy, hold my hand," she'd tell me. "You might fall down." She really takes care of me. She's God's inspiration to me. Grace wrote a poem about Hei Jean when she was just a baby. I want to share my poem with you as she is now.

Hei Jean

Dad
I prayed for you
I prayed for you Dad
I cannot understand
Why you are still in pain.

When I climb up the stairs
When I go down the hills
She runs to me
Hold my hand Dad
You might fall down.

Who will pray today
Hei Jean will pray
Father thank You for today
Please remove Dad's pain

Touch his eyes
Bless baby in Mom's stomach
Thank You for food
Hei Jean will listen
To Mom and Dad
In the name of Jesus
Amen.

Hei Jean where is Jesus
Always in Hei Jean's heart
Who is Jesus
Jesus is Hei Jean's Savior
Dad do you know this song
Love of Jesus sweet and marvelous
We worship and adore Thee
O hail King Jesus
God so loved the world
Hei Jean can sing
Like Dad like Mom.

Hei Jean
Do you love me
I love you
Dad be healthy
To live longer.
Honey, our Lord will come soon
God will keep you
Until that time
Then we will be in heaven together.

Grace and I prayed the same way before Paul (his Korean name is Jung Hyun) was born as we did for Hei Jean. We wanted to pray 1,000 times. We prayed, "O Lord, provide for him a missionary mind, like Paul." We prayed for a boy this time so we could pray this way. When Grace delivered Paul, I think we had prayed about 450 times. The earthquake occurred just a few weeks after he was born, and we had to stop. But we must continue this prayer.

About Paul, he's a genius! Do you know why, Mom? When his diaper is wet, if we do not change it, he will cry. He's a genius! If he is hungry and Grace does not feed him, he will cry. We love this healthy boy. He has four teeth now and he is smiling. He's started to recognize our faces, though I cannot recognize his face because of my eye problem. When he is laughing, that sound really encourages me day by day.

My eye problems and double vision continued, and so I had eye surgery April 1989. The doctors said, "Divergency of both eyes, very wide and deep." They cut my left eye and that made it straight and plain and equal. But still I had double vision. Some people advised me to go to an optical hospital in Seoul to see if anything could be done. So I went there in April 1990. The results of the examination were two: a condition that makes the eyes vibrate and brain nerve trouble. The doctors said there was no cure or any way to treat my eyes. "Prayer is the only thing that can help," they said.

Something else disturbed my studies. I don't know if it was a physical problem or if it had something to do with the brain nerve trouble. For instance, if I was sitting with my professor at his house and we were drinking coffee together and discussing a topic, suddenly I wanted to throw the cup at my professor or break a window. I wanted to shout, to do some crazy thing. Before my brain operation, I never had this kind of trouble.

But now even in the classroom sometimes I had such a desire to stand and shout, to throw out all the tables and chairs. I had such wrong thoughts that sometimes I could not even see my belt in my room for fear that I might commit suicide. The same thoughts occurred about a knife in the kitchen. I told Grace to remove the knife from my eyes. Sometimes I wanted to get out of a running car. I could not understand it. Such crazy, crazy thoughts. Even now I have some of them and cannot always conquer them, sometimes even when I am at the pulpit.

I have to be honest with you, Mom, about my doctoral program. How could I continue to do it with this double vision, the severe pain in my foot, and my physical condition? In my courses I got A's in some subjects and failed in others. One time a faculty member said to me, "If you fail like this one more time, you will be dropped." I received a letter from another one. He told me that my eye problems were no longer a handicap and that it seemed I was really exaggerating my physical condition. This really hurt me, and it totally broke down my heart.

I knew that I was not a faithful student and that they were probably embarrassed in having a student like me in their graduate program. I knew that and that's why I humbly presented myself and said I did not want to take advantage of the program any longer. I did not want to abuse it. Of course, I was very sad when I dropped out. Someday I may know the purpose of this time in my life.

But one thing I know now. God works things out for good for those who love Him. He led me into full-time ministry at the Baguio First Church of the Nazarene when I dropped out of the seminary.

8

FATHER AND SON

(Insights from Stephen)

Last February 1990 I invited my father to hold a revival in my Baguio church, which I began pastoring the year before. He is an evangelist. This was his first trip to a foreign country, so it was an important opportunity for him. One of the elders in my church and I went down to Manila to meet him. As we rode together I shared with him and asked his advice about something that troubled me.

It is a unique custom in my country that wherever we meet our father or our mother, at that place we have to give them the big bow. We have to kneel down, put our two hands to the ground and give a big, big bow. The custom is influenced by Confucianism in our country. My family and almost all Korean families follow this tradition. We are very strict about this. I knew that my father would expect me to give him this big Korean greeting at the airport. It would be embarrassing. I asked the elder, "What shall I do when I see my father at the airport?" I remembered a time in Korea when my eldest brother was in the army. During a vacation when we were at our father's house, construction was going on at our father's church. Unfortunately, at the construction site my brother met my father. It was muddy everywhere. My brother was wearing a nice pressed suit. But he had to put his hands down in the mud, kneel, and give him the big bow. He got all muddy and I was embarrassed.

During vacations at Korea Nazarene Theological College, when I went down to my father's house, I did not inform him at what time I would be arriving at the Mokp'o train station. I knew if he met me there, I would have to give him the big bow. So when I arrived at my parents' city, I called my father from the station. I told him I was at the station and would be arriving home soon. So his house was the first place I'd meet him. I gave him the big bow there. This way I wasn't embarrassed.

So I asked the elder, "What shall I do at the airport? If I give the big bow, people will look and probably laugh and I'll be very embarrassed." He just smiled at me.

At last we were at the airport. It was nighttime. When I saw my father, fortunately, the place was so crowded and there was not even a space to bow down to him. My father said, "Son, you don't need to bow to me right here. I can wait until we arrive at the seminary." So when we arrived there, inside the room I gave him the big bow. Really, Mom, that crowd saved me!

But this kind of greeting is a Korean custom, and my family is very strong on this. My father's word on everything must be respected. My eldest brother always told us, "When there is a black-colored handkerchief, and Father says, 'Son, this handkerchief is white,' how do you answer?"

I said, "I would say, 'It's black, it is not white, Father.'" My brother said, "No, at first you must tell him, 'Yes, Father, it is white. You are right.' After several days you can come back to him and say, 'Father, when I returned to my place, I began wondering if that handkerchief was really white. I think, Father, it was black.'"

Something very important happened when my father was with me in Baguio. First, Mom, I must tell you why it probably happened. My church had a mission outreach school held by a group called Youth with a Mission. They came to our church to train our people, and seven of our young people, attended. I listened to the lectures. One of the strongest emphases was on restitution. I was greatly impressed when I heard about George Lee, one of the teachers and leaders in the mission school.

He had been a waiter in a restaurant. Before he became a Christian, he stole money from the restaurant. After he accepted the Lord, he was under conviction for what he had done. He went to the manager and confessed to him, "When I was working here, I stole some money. Unfortunately, I do not have the money to repay you. But I would like to work without pay until I earn what I stole."

The manager was quite impressed with this man and let him work. Other workers saw the change in George Lee and his beautiful Christian life. Some of them accepted the Lord. I was deeply moved by this story.

When my father was here, I thought of something that happened 15 years ago. I was 13 then. My father was pastoring in a Nazarene church in Mokp'o and the parsonage was in it. When I saw my father's Bible in one room, I opened it. There was money, 500 won. That's about 70 cents now. I stole it and put it in my pocket. It was Sunday. When my father entered the room, he was searching for that money. He asked me, "Son, I placed 500 won here. Have you seen my money? It was my offering."

I told him, "No, Father, I have not seen the money."

He said, "You are the only one who has been in this room."

"Why only me?" I said. "A while ago Mrs. Lee entered this room." She was one of the church members.

My father was really disappointed and frustrated by what I told him. Then it was over.

Later on, I repented. I thought, That's it. I've repented and it's over. I can forget it. But a year later I was reminded of it. I thought, Maybe I didn't completely repent. So I repented again. Two years passed and I was reminded again. I repented again. That happened for 15 years, and I was burdened for what I had stolen.

Now, when my father was at my church for a revival, I asked our missionary students to pray for me. (I told them about my problem first.) I wanted to open up with my father about what I had done. But it seemed like I could not.

Then my father and my family went to the beach. There I was planning to be open with him. We talked for about two hours and had a wonderful time together. But when I wanted to confess to him, the words came up into my throat, into my mouth, to my lips. They stopped right there. I tried over and over again, but I could not tell him.

The last night before my father left for Korea, I had to be open with him. We were in the same room. I could not look straight into his face. I turned off the light so I could not see his face well. Then I said, "Father, I need to be open with you."

"What about?" he asked.

"I stole your money, 500 won, 15 years ago." I shared with him how this had become such a big burden over and over again. Then I turned on the light.

My father's first words were, "You stole 500 won 15 years ago? It was a *big* amount then."

I told him I wanted to pay it back, but he did not want to accept the money. "Please, Father," I insisted, "I want to be free from this."

He held my hand. He started to cry and could not stop. He looked at me and tried to speak but he could not. Later he said, "Son, I don't remember about this. But tell me, where did you learn about what you have just done? This is beautiful. Where did you learn this?"

I told him, "I learned it from my church people."

My father accepted the money. And now, Mom, I am free. I am really free from the burden of 15 years.

Since that time my father and I have become very close. When he returned to Korea, he shared this experience with his church members. He told them, "My son is a beautiful Christian. He is pastoring in heaven."

9

EARTHQUAKE

Stephen gave an almost minute-by-minute account of the disastrous earthquake of 1990: July 16, 4:30 P.M., I entered my room after I finished the treatment of several people. By the way, I was treating with acupuncture that I had learned from a Korean doctor in Manila. This had become a part of my ministry. Every Monday afternoon from 1 to 5 P.M. I did this. I had about 100 patients—Filipinos, Chinese, Koreans, and other nationalities. Of course, this was free. However, I stopped it because of my physical problems and for the sake of my health.

I entered my room and after about five minutes, I heard a terrible sound. The front of our church building was shaking. I was lying on the bed, and it was moved more than two feet and my bookshelves were upside down. Grace was really scared. She put Paul, who at that time was about six weeks old, under the bed.

I asked her, "Where is Hei Jean?"

"I don't know. She's probably outside," she said.

I dashed out and in front of the church, Hei Jean was holding the hand of one of my patients. Right at that time Grace was carrying Paul and she escaped from the building. Our church began collapsing from the third floor. If we had not escaped as soon as we did, we would have been hurt. But by the grace of God, we were able to escape.

This shaking continued more than 30 minutes. All the town became chaos. The first man who came to the church, and this was his first time, said, "Pastor, are you all right?" We sat on the ground in front of the church. We prayed with tears. The shaking continued on and on.

Sherry came to the church. She had lost her first love and was not a faithful church attender. I asked her, "If God would call you right now, are you ready?"

Sherry cried and said, "No, Pastor, I am not really ready. That's why I came here, to die in the church."

"The Lord loves you, Sherry."

"I want to recover my first love, Pastor." She rededicated herself to God. "I am ready to hold the Lord's hand even though He would call me right now," she said.

After that, Mr. and Mrs. Chun, Korean missionaries, came by car. Mrs. Chun works in our church. They are really soldiers of God and comforted the people in the church.

The shaking continued.

One of our young people, Ivie, came and joined us. She was very scared. I asked her, "Ivie, are you ready?"

She cried out, "Pastor, what can I do? I have to repent of so many things. If I would die right now, I would be in hell. What should I do?"

"Let's pray."

We prayed together, "O Lord, You are a God of mercy. Your child, Ivie, is repenting. Now she is accepting the Lord Jesus Christ. Thank You, God."

After a few minutes another of our young people, Lorna, came. When she left her home, her younger brother asked her, "Where are you going?" He and others advised her, "You'd better stay here." But she came.

After three hours our church building collapsed. Fires were everywhere in Baguio. By this time four big hotels had collapsed with many people inside.

Five hours passed. So many streets were destroyed. It was the worst chaos! Many people gathered together in

Parham Park. A Christian there was leading songs. When the third shock came, many were kneeling and crying out to God.

The parsonage was in the basement of the Baguio Church of the Nazarene

A young couple came because they saw the cross on the church. Both accepted the Lord. A Filipino lady also accepted the Lord. Lorna asked us to pray for her sister, a high school teacher in a flooded town. And we prayed for a brother who could not find his wife and two children.

On the Marcos Highway a Korean friend, On Sang Lee, was practicing driving. When we heard that, we prayed for him because that highway is in a very dangerous place. That night he appeared, exhausted and without even his shoes. He said that when he was on the highway, suddenly, it separated. He and his teacher had to leave the car there and walk back to town. People advised them not to. After they crossed the bridge, it fell down. Those who were behind them fell into the separated ground. By the time Mr. Lee passed the last bridge, he had experienced a life-or-death situation 10 times.

The first night we made a fire in front of the church. Church members gathered. Shocks continued about every 20 minutes. We prayed. One of our church trustees came and reported that his two daughters were safe. Now he must check out his relatives in Trinidad, near Baguio.

July 17, 9:30 A.M. It was now 17 hours after the first shock. Shock after shock continued. We heard that one aftershock would be very, very strong, so we were praying, "O Lord, please save us from a strong aftershock."

I hardly knew what to do. I was a young pastor. I looked at the third floor, our social hall. A gas tank was hanging. My office was ruined. On the second floor, where we worship, the roof was down. When I looked at the parsonage in the basement I did not know if it could be repaired. There was no water or electricity.

I told my people in the church, "We must save our food. We will eat just once a day. We will fast. I am the shepherd in front of you. We must be strong. Really, I am not strong. It is only the Lord Jesus Christ who is in me."

I had a terrible headache all night and my eyes hurt. We were able to stay in the church jeepney, which we had bought about three weeks before. That was by the grace of God, and we were thankful because so many people were staying in the streets. It is very cold during the night. We prayed, "O Lord, the people who are dead, the crowds in the streets, whether they are Christians or not, they are all our brothers and sisters. Lord, please comfort the hurting families. Please hold them."

We were concerned, too, for a Korean minister and his family. At the time of the first shock yesterday, Pastor Yu and his wife went to their children's school to get them. We wondered how they were. We also wondered about a lady pastor, a short-term missionary from Korea, who was living on the second floor of an apartment building. She was ministering in a Campus Crusade for Christ conference. About 3,000 were there. A few days ago the wife of the director came and asked us to pray for them. Now, we prayed, "Father, protect them. And, Lord, may all of us be ready when You call us."

July 18, 11 A.M. Just a while ago there was another aftershock. It was 43 hours after the first shock. The strongest building in Baguio, the Hyatt Hotel, and Baguio Park Hotel fell down just like they had been made of straw. Even at the University of Baguio many classrooms where students were studying were destroyed. Every street, every park, was crowded. It was raining and people were standing outside. They had no choice. They had to stay there overnight.

We heard that Pastor Yu's family and the lady pastor were safe. But Rev. Choi, who went to Agasena, about two hours from Baguio, was returning home and he had to stop on a country road. A big bus was nearly covered by the mountain and all the people inside were dead. On another road both sides were full of dead bodies.

We were wondering when the shocks would be over. Someone said the last one would be 72 hours after the first. People were really in chaos because they could not get food. Even the gas stations were closed. A lady carried two kilograms of rice to the church this morning.

My heart was full of confusion for my family. We had temporary shelter in front of our church. We cooked there. Church members brought rice and vegetables. They took good care of me and my family. They were really concerned about me because I am a foreigner and handicapped. I thought, I am the one who is supposed to comfort you because I am the shepherd.

A while ago Pastor and Mrs. Chun suggested that we should visit Tuba, a mountain area. Ten of our church members come from this place. If they were in difficulty, we must bring them to the church.

July 19, 11:30 A.M. Another shock. It was 67 hours from the first shock. We were getting used to them now. Early this morning there were four strong shocks in Baguio, but we are *in* our Lord Jesus Christ. Yesterday afternoon when we were preparing to go to Tuba, people advised us to take emergency food in case we were not able to get there. Hei Jean, Grace, and Paul went with us. When we arrived at Tuba, a policeman told us nobody had been hurt there. Our hearts were so grateful.

The road was destroyed and many were sick there. But when they heard about the destruction of our church, they said, "Pastor, we will see you in church on Sunday." So many people had gathered, and they prepared food for us. Most of the market was closed, but they opened a small door so the people could get food. The price of the items did not go up. It stayed the same. The Filipinos are honest, and I love them. They held my hand, and we prayed together.

The radio was still telling us the last aftershock had not yet passed. It would probably be at 4:00 this afternoon. After that time a long-distance call was possible. But I would have to wait at the place more than five hours before I could make one. This morning a lady came to the church to hand me 100 pesos. She said, "I'm praying for you, Pastor." She had seen us one Sunday several months ago. We met Lorna's sister, the high school teacher who was in the flooded area. Her boyfriend went down there, and they hiked back to Baguio. They were on the road more than 15 hours. The house of the relatives of a member of my church was destroyed. Four people were inside dead. The funeral service, he said, would be today.

We prayed, "O Lord, please help us. Please remove the last aftershock." My people and I prayed together. I experienced continually their help. They cooked bananas, rice, and vegetables for us. We wondered how long we should stay in this temporary shelter. A month? Two months? One thing was clear. If I had to solve all the problems by myself, I would surely fail. But He who is in us is able to save us and give us the victory. And through this experience there will be great fruit, spiritual fruit, and we will be His true disciples.

I began writing this Sunday's sermon, "Is God Still a God of Love?" It is true. He is still a God of love . . .

That same day Stephen wrote a letter to Dr. Rench in Manila:

Dear Dr. Rench:

We were able to escape when the building was falling down. I was outside with our four-year-old, and Grace got the baby out. No one in our church is seriously injured though some of them were working in the destroyed hotels and other buildings. Now they are searching for survivors or involved in funerals for relatives.

We are staying outside, cooking outside. We decided to eat once a day only since it is very difficult to buy food. There is no electricity, no water. The church people are helping us in various ways.

I am sure God will allow us victories moment by moment through this disaster. Those who came to church were praying and singing together. Seven of them accepted the Lord in the midst of the disaster. My sermon title this Sunday will be, "Is God Still a God of Love?"

From the shoulder of God,
Pastor Stephen Kim

Stephen later reported to Dr. Rench concerning his church's ministry following the earthquake:

Baguio First Church of the Nazarene
4 Gov. Bado Dangwa Street
Guidad, Baguio
August 20, 1990

Dr. George Rench
P.O. Box 179
Greenhills 1502
Metro Manila

Dear Dr. Rench:

I greet you in the name of our Lord Jesus Christ.

The Baguio First Church of the Nazarene building was badly damaged by the killer earthquake, but the church is still alive in the Lord. Praise God for that!

We are undergoing tough times, especially just after the earthquake, but I'm indeed grateful to God for the brethren who supported us morally, financially, and spiritually. One of our supporters is the Nazarene Mission. God has comforted us and is continually comforting us through His people during our desperate times. We were comforted to comfort others. God enabled us to share the blessings we received with other people who are not members of our church.

When I went down to Manila, I met a Korean Christian Medical team headed by Dr. and Mrs. En-Je Jo. They volunteered to come with me to Baguio and be of help to our people. I accompanied them to the different areas where they rendered free services and medicines. They are not Nazarenes, but they were willing to work in Baguio under the banner of the Church of the Nazarene. Before they left for Korea, they donated relief rice, which we call "Korean Love Rice." They donated some more so we decided to share the blessings with others who are needy.

Distributing "Korean Love Rice"

The young people, together with some of our elders, conducted surveys in the affected areas like San Carlos Heights, Fairview, Sunnyside, and Lucnab, after which they distributed the relief rice and free medicines. Along with the distribution of relief, the gospel was also shared and many accepted Christ as their Lord and Savior.

After a few days, my brother, Elijah Kim, and his friends came all the way from Korea. God had touched their hearts, and they brought along with them free medicines, which we are now giving to the needy. We are also able to acquire anticholera and typhoid vaccines through the efforts of Brother Timothy Chun, who went to Korea and returned some days ago. These free vaccines were donated by a Christian church in Korea. Yesterday our nurses started giving immunization to our church members and nonchurch members. Today they are still continuing with the vaccination.

Sister Nora Peligman, our CLASS [then called Christian Life and Sunday School] chairman, who took charge of the Evangelistic Team from our church, will give you the details of our activities since the earthquake happened. According to her, there were about 1,000 to whom the group had ministered. This is excluding our church members.

There is a great spiritual revival in our church. In fact, the Bible study group in Trancoville that used to meet once a week is now having nightly meetings to worship the Lord and learn from His Word. Dr. En-Je Jo, my brother, Elijah, and some of his Korean friends had the chance to share God's Word (during separate meetings) in that Bible study area. We were all blessed during the meetings. I'm also glad to tell you that some of the church members who stopped coming to church for a long time are now returning to the Lord.

Thank you for informing us about possible job opportunities at LNBC. [Campus buildings were damaged during the earthquake.] I, myself, will be participating in the work, maybe as a painter or whatever job is available in accordance with my capabilities. I announced the job opportunity to the congregation. I'm sure those who are available will also participate.

Thank you also for standing by us in our desperate times. May God bless you and your family.
In Christ's service,
Rev. Stephen Kim, Pastor

Nora Peligman's letter to Dr. Rench included some of what Stephen wrote. Parts of it that did not are as follows:

I am happy to let you know that since we experienced the earthquake, God gave us the grace to focus on His great mercy and love instead of magnifying our misery and just wait for relief. Thank God that even in the midst of distress and troubles, we can still glorify Him and share His love with other people.

A few days after the earthquake, Brother Pen Boco, a member of our Board of Trustees, led the young people in clearing up the falling debris in our church. We also organized an evangelistic team that acted as a survey team . . . The situations of the people in these areas touched us a lot. We do experience sufferings, but their suffering is greater than ours . . .

Thank God for every opportunity given to us to serve Him. Not a single day was wasted. Before we went out to survey or distribute relief goods, we always started our activities with a time of worship in the church. The members of our team, which is composed mostly of young people, enjoyed every activity of the day. Though we had to hike a lot, eat our lunch late, and go home very tired, we were still glad because we were serving the Lord. We can see how God is blessing us through our activities . . .

A last September report by Steve Weber, international coordinator of Nazarene Compassionate Ministries, gives an account of the results of the earthquake, especially related to the Church of the Nazarene. It was written in conjunction with thanking members of Bethany First Church of the Nazarene for contributing to the Nazarene Hunger and Disaster Fund:

. . . On July 16, an earthquake measuring 7.7 on the Richter scale rocked the city of Cabanatuan in the Philippines at 4:26 P.M. Three minutes later, at 4:29 P.M. an 8.0 jolt centered in Baguio shook the area violently. These two powerful earthquakes left over 1,650 people dead and another 1,000 people missing. Over 3,000 people were injured, and more than 130,000 are left homeless . . .

The damage in life and property is great. At Baguio Church of the Nazarene [Stephen's church] 45 families have lost their jobs and/or homes, in addition to all of their belongings. In Camp Dangwa and Pico, 11 more Nazarene families have lost their homes, jobs, and belongings. Food is scarce, and prices are increasing throughout the city. Needs for food, medicine, and other items throughout the area remain critical. In addition, at least five Nazarene churches and the Luzon Nazarene Bible College were damaged.

. . . Nazarene Compassionate Ministries is providing food, medicine, and other urgently needed items to those in need. And long after all the news cameras are gone, we will still be there helping the people with the tremendous recovery and construction needs that plague them. Pastor Stephen Kim, who escaped with his family from a collapsing building, reports that several people have already accepted the Lord in the midst of this disaster. Together with Pastor Kim, we are certain that "God will allow us victories moment by moment throughout this disaster" as we reach out with the love of our Lord Jesus Christ.

The killer earthquake, Mom, brought about a crisis in my life, a kind I had not experienced before. This was the first and biggest crisis since Grace and I married. We had to stay in the church jeepney for eight days with our two children. Paul was only six weeks old, and Hei Jean was four years. We had to cook outside; we had no water or electricity. And aftershocks were occurring continually. There were 624 of them.

People from the Luzon Nazarene Bible College suggested we stay there. The McMahons from LNBC came one Sunday and offered us a place there and advised us to move to the college. I was there only a little while because my people came often to the church, and I had to be there. This was what I thought, Mom. Their pastor must be there to see his people and encourage them, one by one.

I was struggling between two different kinds of advice. One was from my minister father in Korea. When I called him, he said, "Son, you die in the church." And my mother told me, "It is very important for the pastor to be with the people. Do not leave the church." So for the Koreans, it is God first; ministry, second; family, third. But for Westerners it is God first, then family before ministry.

My friends and my family in Korea advised me to stay with the church. And so I stayed in the church. Grace had a really difficult time with the children, especially going around in Baguio where there was cholera and typhoid. She asked me to accompany them to Manila, by airplane. I told her, "Grace, really I cannot leave my church." I asked her to stay with me. She asked me again to go with her. American missionaries advised me to go with her and take care of my family. That went before my ministry. I really could not do it and thought that I was right. I had to send her alone with our two little children. I stayed alone in Baguio.

That was a very severe crisis. Grace had to stay in Manila without my care. She had to transfer from place to place because she did not want to touch other people's privacy. She had no place to stay even. She needed my care. But I ignored my family and stayed concerned about our church and ministry.

After about a month I made a quick trip to Manila to get medical help for my people. I met Grace and told her, "I have to return immediately to Baguio to help our people." I went with a Korean medical team and we took medicine, vaccines, and rice.

Grace was deeply, deeply hurt. And even I was hurt, Mom, because I asked Grace to return with me. I knew I could not survive by myself without my wife's care. But she stayed in Manila.

I continued to struggle over the differing advice people gave me. My brother, Elijah, has the same concept I was taught—always to consider first the church. He is a Presbyterian minister in Seoul. About a month after the first shock he came to the Philippines, did visitation in Baguio for me, and preached two Sundays in my church. He helped me greatly. He called Grace in Manila and asked her, "Why are you there? You're supposed to be in Baguio."

The first night Elijah slept here, another shock occurred. He fell from his bed. He called Grace again and told her, "Grace, I realize it is not the proper time for you to be here. So please stay there and I will pay for your house rent there, and other expenses I will pay. So please do not come back to Baguio."

After the work of the mission teams was finished, I went down to Manila again. That was the time Grace's heart had already departed from me. And also my heart had departed from her. When I was with the Renches, Mrs. Rench said to me, "Stephen, please take care of your family. Do everything Grace asks of you. Please accept her advice 100 percent."

That was very different advice from what my friends in Korea gave me. I went to Grace and asked her to return with me to Baguio. We had family devotions together and that's the time we opened everything. Grace shared with me how deeply hurt she had been. I had been hurt too, I told her. By God's grace we were able to reunite and we returned to Baguio.

Later on, I realized that the family must be prior to the ministry. It must be that way. It took me a long time to realize the truth of this. When the apostle Paul wrote about the Christian life in Ephesians, he was very clear about this. But in our country, this is not true. The ministry must always be before family.

10

BAGUIO CHURCH OF THE NAZARENE

I must explain to you, Mom, how I came to this church in Baguio. While I was studying for my doctor's degree at the seminary here, our First Church of the Nazarene had no pastor because the one they had resigned. He left for the United States. My Filipino friend, Tereso Casino, a faculty member at Luzon Nazarene Bible College, talked to me. He was a pulpit minister at the church, and he invited me to be another pulpit minister. So I went because of his invitation. Before I went there, I attended the college church at LNBC.

By July I was holding the Sunday morning and evening revival meeting. I held the revival for 10 Sundays. Then I became the resident pastor of the church. In October I became the full-time pastor when I dropped out of the doctoral program.

The pastoral ministry in the Philippines is so different from that in Korea. This is because the culture in the Philippines is entirely different. You see, in the Filipino church we follow the Nazarene *Manual*. At the General Assembly some Korean traditions having to do with our culture were accepted. For instance, in Korea we do not have a board of trustees, but we have elders. They are called *jangros*. *Jangros* are very strong in Korean society.

Once they become elders, or stewards, they continue for a lifetime. There is no election every year. There are both positives and negatives about this system. When I became the pastor of the Baguio church, this was the first thing I noticed.

Another thing I found different was that people were not keeping the time. For instance, our morning service starts about 10:00 or 10:10 and finishes about 11:40. Some of our people even come about 11:00. I was really struggling. Why were these people coming this late? After the service this person who came late would tell me, "I'm sorry I was late." But it seemed by her face that she was not really sorry, but was just saying that. I told her it was OK and expected her to come on time the next Sunday. But at 11:00 she would come again. The same time! It's just like a sickness.

I was struggling a lot because of this. How could I get my people to come on time? I talked with a Filipino about this. He was studying at APNTS. He told me what one of his professors said about this matter of time. He said, "Suppose our meetings are from 9:00 to 11:00. For the German people, if they come at 9:05, they're late five minutes. For the Americans, if they come between 8:55 and 9:05, it is OK. But for the Filipinos, they can arrive anytime from 9:00 to 11:00. It is all right."

He said Germans, Americans, and even Koreans are controlled by their watches. They're products of mechanism. But Filipinos are event-centered people. This is a higher value than that of the other three countries. He advised me, "Do not blame them, Pastor, even though they are late."

Since I talked with him, I am grateful that even though they come late, they come. I had to change. Before, I said, "You must keep the time. Coming late is a sickness you have." I don't do that now.

We had overnight prayer meetings every Friday, just like in Korea. In these meetings a few Koreans joined us.

We had about 25 or 30 people. We Koreans, you probably noticed, when we pray, we pray so loud. Sometimes very loud and for a long time.

We Koreans did this at APNTS in our early morning prayer meetings. Our Filipino friends came to us and said to me, "Brother, last night we studied until late and now we have to have sleep." Another time some Filipinos asked, "Why do Koreans pray so loud?" I answered them like this: "Sorry, my brothers. The reason why we have to pray so loud is because an empty can makes the most noise. See, we are just empty cans. I'm sorry."

Then they said they were sorry about complaining so often. They didn't complain anymore.

In the Philippines the secret to successful pastoral ministry and church relationships is openness. Pastors in Korea cannot be this way. For instance, I have this pain in my right foot and I ask a church member, "Would you come here and pray for me?" And I ask him to lay his hand on my foot and pray. This is impossible in Korea. A pastor never asks a layperson to lay his hands on his body and pray. That is never, never done in Korea. If he did, the member would say, "Pastor, I am just a layperson. How can I lay my hands on your body and pray?" He would not accept my request.

I must share with you, Mom, some things about my ministry related to healing. I was leading family devotions in the home of one of our church members. This woman was crying out about something she didn't understand. One of her sons is a doctor in the United States. He had polio, and her grandson has bladder trouble. She questioned me, "Why, Pastor, why have all of these things happened to me? Sometimes I question whether God is a God of love. What is the reason so many righteous people suffer?"

I said to her, "If you are complaining because of your misfortunes, how much more do I have reason to complain. But, really, God has a divine purpose, which we cannot understand now. Someday we will know."

I do not know why God heals some and not others. He has given to my father a special gift of healing. When he held a revival meeting in my church, God performed miracles of healing. Thirteen were healed by the grace of God through his ministry. I was overwhelmed by this.

People around me advised me to keep quiet about the healing service. They said, "Do not talk about it to the American missionaries in Manila. If you do, they might misunderstand and think you are a charismatic. So please be careful and do not say anything."

So when I visited APNTS and missionaries asked, "How was your father's revival meeting?" I simply said, "It was good; it was really good."

That's the way it was until I met the Gordon Gibsons there. Rev. Gibson was the construction coordinator. His wife explained to me that healing services in the United States are strong. I was surprised. Then I shared with them that God healed 13 people during my father's revival meeting. They were happy to hear that. When I told them I had been cautioned not to talk about it, they said, "In the United States in the healing services in the Church of the Nazarene, they even apply oil." Mom, I need to know more about the Church of the Nazarene, especially about healing.

I would like to say one more thing about healing. When I was an associate pastor of the Church of the Nazarene in Ch'onan City, one of our church pastors, Rev. Yung, suffered from asthma. From late autumn until midwinter he had to be treated at the hospital. He had to spend about $3,000 a year for medical expenses. He invited me to have family devotions at his house. He asked me, "Pastor Kim, will you pray for me? It is time for me to go to the hospital. I need your prayers."

I called all of the family members and one by one we prayed. I laid my hand on him and prayed. That was a wonderful family devotion. Afterward when we were at the door, Rev. Yung said, "When we were having family devotions, I experienced the presence of the Holy Spirit."

After one week from that time he had no more asthma. When he was checked at the hospital, the doctor told him, "It has clearly disappeared."

It was he who announced to the congregation, "Pastor Kim prayed for me, and I was healed."

I was really proud of this event. I told myself, "Now I have spiritual ability. I carry this ability in my pocket." When anyone in the church was seeking to be healed, I said, "No problem. When I prayed for Pastor Yung, he was healed." I thought I could just take the healing ability out of my pocket and apply it.

My wife was concerned. I told her, "Never mind, don't worry. God has given to me this ability." After this time I prayed for other sick people. But miracles never, never happened. They were not healed. I was troubled and wondered what was wrong. Later on, I realized it was my wrong attitude. The power to heal is God's. The ability is God's. Whenever I need that power, I must ask Him, "O Lord, I am nothing but for You in my heart. Would You come with Your mighty power and heal this person?" It's from God; it's not in my pocket. I must ask Him every time. It took several years for me to realize this.

I have learned many other things about the ministry since that time. An experience I had here not long ago taught me something important. I must renew concern for a compassionate ministry. My family and I were in a Nazarene church at Bicol, 19 hours distant from Baguio. I held classes in discipleship training and Brother Tereso Casino held an expository preaching seminar. Bicol is a poor town. Only a few radios and perhaps no TVs. The people have no money to buy newspapers. They do not know what's going on inside their country or around the world. Even the pastor has no watch. So many pastors don't have watches. That's why they preach one or two hours. They must depend on their wives to give the sign to stop. Before I left I gave my watch to the pastor.

In this area are many typhoons, 25 to 30 every year. The people are victimized by them. That's one reason they are so poor. They want to go to church, but they have no money for transportation. Always I think of the people in this area. Whenever I have opportunity I get watches and send them. I'd like to send a radio also because it would be so good there. But I cannot. I have a heavy heart because of this. I pray, "Lord, help me to be a compassionate pastor."

I really like being pastor of this Filipino church here in Baguio. Even though I have been here only a few months, I can see how God is using me. The people like me and I like them. What I think is this. I must not try to bring them up to my standards in education, etc. If I try, I will fail. I had rather go down to their standards. I will hold their hands, and hand in hand and little by little we will do better. But if I insist on keeping my authority and bringing them up to my standards, I will fail in every area. Mom, I am sending you a copy of my pastoral report I gave at the Central Luzon District Assembly in March 1990. I was proud to give it.

PASTORAL REPORT
Central Luzon District Assembly
March 1990

I am so happy to be a member of Central Luzon District in the Philippines. Thank you for accepting me as one of your coworkers. My heart is full of joy and peace. Hallelujah!

The first thing I realized in our church was the five years district debt, that is since 1985. I encouraged our board members with these words: "Why don't we risk together? I will not receive the salary until we pay the whole district debt. Let us work an easy decision." Several times I had nothing to eat and I fasted. But our people started to bring rice, meat, and vegetables. They were willing to sacrifice themselves day by day. Praise the Lord! We were able to pay 1987, 1989, and this year's district budget. Our church is the first church that paid the district dues. God lifted us up to pay 80% of the whole amount. We are willing to pay the rest and clear up the church history, although I am now receiving my salary.

The amount is indeed bigger than 1 million U.S. dollars because this salary carries the love, concern, heart, and even the tears of our people. At present I am living in the most beautiful parsonage in the Philippines, with a water heater, church refrigerator, both 110 and 220 voltages. The parsonage is really a beautiful repainted nest of God. There are three freedoms in the parsonage. The people are free to fix their own coffee, free to wash the dishes, and free to bring something.

It was the last Preachers' Meeting, 1989. I was greatly challenged by Dr. Stephen Manley's message. He said that it is now time to go out, to be concerned for people outside of our church. Our church became a mission-minded church as we are supporting one of the sister churches of Loo Church in the mountains. We are praying to support 12 churches in the next three years. This is one of our visions.

Youth outreach in Bontoc

We are also holding a Mission Bridge School training program for outreach after the training is over. The outreach will be done by the third week of April. Our church had also produced three missionaries sent by Youth with a Mission. One is in Singapore, another is in Switzerland, and still another in Bontoc. [This is in the mountains some distance north of Baguio.] We are receiving their mission report as their home church. Yes, we are called to spread the gospel of our Lord Jesus Christ—the message of salvation and entire sanctification to unreached people.

Our theme for 1990 is "Arise, shine" (Isa. 60:1). The Friday night prayer meetings bind us together in the love of Christ as we share our struggles and pray together. It is also my joy to say that the lovely care through the pastor's shower, which is taken the first Sunday of every month, is a great, great blessing. The relationship of the churches in Zone 7 has greatly improved. The Pico, Camp Dangwa, and College churches joined together and contributed a lot during our last revival. We will work together in unity. All of us are willing to build up the Body of Christ over the gaps and hindrances. Hallelujah!

Once one of our elders confessed with tears, "We love you, Pastor Kim, not because you are a foreigner. We love you, Pastor Kim, not because you took a doctoral study. We love you, Pastor Kim, because you are our pastor."

Indeed, it is no longer I who have done things but Christ who is in me for I am "crucified with Christ; and it is no longer I who live, but Christ lives within me; and the life which I now live in the flesh I live by faith in the Son of God, who loved me, and delivered Himself up for me." [Gal. 2:20, NASB]

Respectfully submitted,
Rev. Stephen Kim
(Pastor)

I am so thankful to have wonderful leaders, like Dr. George Rench to help me. He writes to me over and over again and answers all of my letters. When I wrote him a letter about the big earthquake July 16, he wrote to me at once. Mom, I want to share it with you:

July 23, 1990

Rev. Stephen Kim
c/o MCPO Box 556
1299 Makati
Metro Manila

Dear Rev. Kim:

Your note to me concerning the earthquake has just been handed to me. I was deeply moved as I read about your experience. Praise God He has protected so many of our people who could have been easily killed or hurt including your wife and baby. God is good and as you no doubt preached about it on Sunday, is still a God of love.

We don't understand why good people are hurt and suffer but we know they do. It is His special grace and favor that protects and watches over us during times like this. I know that many will wonder and be asking why didn't God protect every Christian during the earthquake. Though as far as I have learned none of our Nazarenes have been seriously hurt, yet we know that many good and godly people didn't escape injury or death. The problem of pain and suffering will go unanswered until this old world is no more. As the songwriter said, "We will understand it better by and by."

This morning, I talked with Rev. Danny McMahan, and he informed me that you and Grace and family were staying with them. He was glad that you were there with them. I want you to know that earlier today, I phoned Korea and left a message that you and your family were safe and had not been hurt, but that your church had suffered severe damage.

Wouldn't it be great to have the Korean church rally to this tragic event and help you rebuild the Baguio church!

Rev. Williams was in my office this morning, and he will be bringing some economic assistance to help you and

the church. Our Nazarenes around the world will do all they can to help our family in Baguio First Church. Please assure your people of our prayers, love, and concern.
Sincerely,
George E. Rench

Dr. Rench's letter encouraged me. Several weeks later I was really confused and discouraged. Probably, I tried to do too many things. I became involved in social welfare because of the earthquake. My people needed help, and I was able to get relief supplied from Manila and help from Nazarene Compassionate Ministries and to administer it more than once. I was busy taking care of my people and some others. I was becoming an expert at it!

At the same time I lost the zeal and enthusiasm for preparing sermons and preaching. I couldn't handle this ministry and the social welfare at the same time. So I wrote to Dr. Rench. I poured out everything, like this: "Doctor, I don't think I can do two things at once. Maybe I should quit my ministry. I'm not being a good shepherd. There were many people who came to church after the earthquake. I was supposed to visit them, take care of them, and feed them spiritually. But I really cannot because of my physical condition. What a shepherd I am! Sometimes I even have a fear of having a bigger congregation because I want to relax. If I had a bigger one, I would be in trouble. I'm not a good shepherd, so I think I should quit."

Again Dr. Rench wrote to me and greatly encouraged me. Mom, I must share this letter with you also:

November 2, 1990
Rev. Stephen Kim
4 Gov. Bado Dangwa Street
Guidad
2600 Baguio

Dear Brother Stephen:

I have received your letter of October 17 in which you have shared your burdens and poured out your heart.

Stephen, I am praying God will bless, help, and strengthen you. All of these feelings of inadequacy, helplessness, and weariness are from Satan and have no basis of fact.

All of us have been blessed and encouraged to see how wise, strong, and dynamic your leadership has been through the earthquake and its aftermath. The Lord has indeed used you, and you have proven to be a dedicated, faithful shepherd to your people. I am convinced no one else could have done as much for them as you have done.

May God himself minister to you and Grace these days. Please be assured of our continued support and prayers.

Sincerely,

George E. Rench

God did come and minister to us. Deep in my heart I have a strong determination to be a faithful shepherd. Now I am preparing a long-range plan for our church, for the next five years. I will present it to the board soon. Our visions, Mom, like supporting 12 churches in the next three years (you read that in my pastoral report) must come to reality, by God's grace. I pray that God's plan for our church will be fulfilled. Grace and I want that for our lives too. He is preparing us for our future ministry with the handicapped in our country.

During the last few years I have been reminded time after time that God's grace is sufficient for me. That was true when I had brain surgery and just a few months ago when I had eye surgery. I wrote a poem that is not only about the past but also about the present and the future.

My Grace Is Sufficient for You
When people are blessed through my message
When I am far from Thy will
When I am struggling

The pain is always there
Striking pain by a gimlet piercing
My right foot weakest part of my body
Imposing leg-screw torture
Nine months of painful injections
Yet the message behind the pain
My grace is sufficient for you.

Ah
This is a thumb mark of our Lord Jesus Christ
This is a seal of the Holy Spirit on my back
Two sometimes three hours of
Massaging till I fall asleep
Thy hands are so gracious to me.

Now I am willing to boast about it
Just today is great to me
All the people I meet are precious to me
Now I am willing to uncover this pain.

My teeth are on edge
My face covered with perspiration
My head has only a dim consciousness
But I can see the light beyond this pain
A brightened sea only I behold
A smell of a beautiful red rose
A hopeful world in my hands!

My doctor said
Divergency 16
Nystagmus (brain nerve trouble)
Operation impossible
Brain tumor
Fear complex since my other brain surgery
Tube from the brain to the bladder
Double sometimes triple vision.

This is it *but*
My grace is sufficient for you

Living today with unmerited love
It's not I anymore
But only the treasure in this vessel
Controlling my life.

I am afflicted in every way
But not crushed
Persecuted
But not forsaken
Struck down
But not destroyed
Always carrying about in the body
The death of Jesus
That the life of Jesus
May also be manifested in my body.

His grace *is* sufficient for me!

11

CULTURAL DIFFERENCES

The Filipino culture, Mom, is quite unique. Really, two cultures exist. One is totally uncivilized; the other is modern. In the mountain area, if we go up higher from Baguio, we find the first culture. Thousands of years of history have not changed the people much. They have a number of quite different customs depending on the area. For instance, in one area, funeral ceremonies take place near a fire. People dance around it. The dead body is near the fire too. This custom still exists.

The modern culture in the cities was influenced by Spain and other parts of the Western world. The Philippines, I think, were conquered by Spain and later, by America for a short time, and then the Japanese. We can see the influence of these foreign countries upon the Filipinos.

Ever since I've been in the Philippines, I have struggled so many times because of the cultural differences. We Koreans don't understand them. For instance, when some Koreans visited rural areas here, they saw farmers sleeping under the trees with their cows. They are called carabao. One of them asked me, "Why are Filipinos so lazy?"

"They are not lazy," I answered.

"We saw farmers sleeping under trees at noonday. They're supposed to be working," he said. "What do you say to this?"

I told him, "The carabao need some time to rest, like at noontime. The farmers respect and take care of the carabao like their family members. So they rest also for the sake of the carabao." Many Koreans perhaps would force them to work, but the Filipinos, they cannot.

Another thing, Mom, when you were in Korea you know we were always in a hurry. We cannot persevere truly, even in traffic. When there is a yellow light, we are supposed to wait until the light turns green. But people cannot wait, so they run on the yellow light. If the car in front will not go, the car behind will horn and horn and horn. In Korea we are always in a hurry, but that is our culture. That's why we commit so many mistakes. The Filipinos are secure and so can persevere. We must learn this.

I did not realize this at first, but it is true. In the Philippines, the driving law is very general. In Korea, it is very strict. But the accident rate here is lower than in Korea, though there are plenty of cars. This may be the reason: even though Filipinos break the law in passing and making U-turns in a prohibited area, the drivers never, never get angry. I have observed this. They are permitted to carry out their own wishes about driving and don't get angry. I am impressed by their behavior.

In the Philippines family ties are very strong. For example, if a family member becomes rich, the others come to live with them. In America this doesn't seem to be possible, for they never want to be touched by others. They want their privacy. Privacy is very important, but in the Philippines privacy is almost nothing. The family member who is rich just expects others of the family to live with him.

Of course, family ties in Korea are very strong also, so our two cultures have some similarities. Both countries have national days that honor the family. In Korea, we have *Chusok* in the autumn. You have a Thanksgiving Day in the United States. Some say *Chusok* is the Korean Thanksgiving Day. I think this is the wrong expression. It is a very important holiday when the entire family has a reunion. They visit their ancestors' tombs, prepare food there, and offer it in a ceremony. It's a pagan practice.

All Souls' Day in the Philippines is about the same as *Chusok*. The families also come together, visit their forefathers' tombs, offer food, and have a ceremony.

In Korea another important national day when families come together is Lunar New Year's Day. Every year it changes. Last year it was February 16. This year it was February 9. Sometimes, it's the last of January. We all gather together. We kneel down on the ground and give the big bow to our parents. The parents give children money according to their age. In my childhood on that day I would go around and around and visit many families. I got up early to do this. I would kneel and give the big bow. Then they would give me money. That was our great interest, to see how many families we could visit and how much money we could get.

In Korea, there are special days for celebration of family members, old and young. For instance, when a parent has a 60th birthday, called *hwangap,* there is a big celebration. It is very important, for this is the day when a person completes the 60-year cycle of the oriental zodiac. If you live this long, you have lived much and you have no regrets when you die. My father will celebrate *hwangap* June 6, 1991. His sons and daughter will all be with him to give him the big bow and honor him.

Also, when a baby is 100 days old, there is a big celebration. All of the members of the family and friends are invited to a big feast with special foods. Rings are given to the baby. There is much rejoicing because the baby has survived this long. It used to be that many babies died before this time. This is the original reason for the celebration. Nowadays another reason is given too—celebration of the baby's first birthday. We count the nine months the baby is in the womb and add 100 days. So that makes a year. A Korean child is two years old when an American child is one.

Mom, about children, here is another cultural difference. When Jo Edlin came to my house in Baguio, I asked my daughter, "Hei Jean, who are you?"

She answered, "I am the daughter of Rev. Kim."
Jo asked me, "Did you teach her to say that?"
"Yes," I said.

She looked at me as if I were something strange. I could not understand why she was looking at me like that. If I teach my child "I'm Rev. Kim," Americans feel there is a big, big gap between father and daughter. But in Korea as early as possible we teach this formal way.

In Korea, we have a tradition about naming children. For example, both the first name [surnames are given first] and the middle name are kept in a family. Only sons are affected by this custom; girls are not. My name is Kim Sung Kap. My four brothers all have "Kap" for their middle names. Nowadays some Koreans, especially Christians, are violating some of our traditions about naming their children. My friends here in Baguio gave their boy a name that means "creation." A boy in another family was given a name that means "honesty." I was also planning to do this and give my boy, Jung Hyun, a Bible name. But my father was very strong against this. He said, "Son, you are a Nazarene pastor. You must follow our heritage." I'm not a brave enough person in our society to change. Some are almost cast out from their families because they violate their heritage, but they were brave enough to do it.

Mom, this is about something different that I witnessed in the Philippines—the coup d'etat. Over and over again since I have been in the Philippines they have occurred. They're strange here. They mean something different than they do in Korea. In Manila when there is a coup d'etat, there is one broadcasting nationwide. I asked the people, "Who won? The government or the rebels?" They said, "Nobody." Since this is a nationwide broadcast, neither the government or those in the coup d'etat want it. The station explains what is going on, and someone favoring the government will come to them and campaign for the government. The next moment someone from the coup d'etat. This happens on the same broadcasting. That I cannot understand, but in a way I do.

Coup d'etats in Manila are almost like games. When shooting goes on, people watching them run and hide behind a building or something. After the shooting is over, they come out and cheer, some for the government and some for the coup d'etat. They give names of professional basketball players to those fighting and cheer for them. It's like a game. It's not a game, people are dying. It's never that way in Korea, never, never . . .

There are many other differences in our cultures. For instance, the feeling toward pastors in Korea and the Philippines, I think, is different. In Korea more respect is given to the pastors. Whether people are Christians or non-Christians, if they know I am a minister they look up to me and treat me as someone special. The last time I was in Korea, I was sitting in the bus station with a Korean friend. He was holding my crutches. When he called me "Rev. Kim," the people surrounding me looked at me with a different attitude and invited me to sit in a better place.

Respect is given in Korea to pastors because of the high position they hold. They have high moral standards. They do not smoke or drink or have sex scandals. In our Korean church history, for the last 100 years there may have been some unknown pastors who might have had sex scandals. But for the many major leaders, I have not heard of even one who had one. In the Philippines there is a second chance for the pastor who is involved in a sex scandal, but in my country there is no second chance. If he wants to pastor, he must get out of the country.

Respect for pastors is one of the two important reasons Korean girls are now wanting to marry men who plan to become pastors. About 10 years ago at Ewha Girls' University in Seoul, a survey was taken. The first question was, What profession would you like the man you marry to have? In a list of 30 professions the top choices were law, medicine, and government. The ministry was No. 28. Last year the same survey was taken. This time the ministry was No. 1 on the list. Do you know why, Mom? First of all, because of the financial ability of the pastor. It has improved very much over the last 10 years. Pastors nowadays even have their own cars. But something else is very important too—their high moral standards and high standards of education for their children.

Mom, I want to tell you about one thing that I realize is very important when talking about differences in culture. Something that is fair in one culture can be considered very unfair in other cultures. Some things fair in the United States are not considered fair in the Philippines and Korea. And some things fair in these countries are considered very much unfair in the United States. For instance, in the United States you keep animals and feed them so many nice and expensive foods. Your living standard is different from Asia's. That is the beauty of America and of the abundant life, financially. In the eyes of Filipinos, that is very unfair, keeping animals and feeding them expensive foods. Several Sundays ago during our Sunday School class, a teacher told us she had been in the United States. What surprised her, she said, was that Americans were treating animals like human beings. In her eyes this was unfair because there was not even enough food in the Philippines to feed human beings.

Mom, in Asia we eat dog meat. I eat it too. Now, you'll probably say, "You stop calling me 'Mom' anymore because of that!" I'm sorry, Mom, however, it is our culture. This custom is very unfair in the United States, but it is fair here. Because of several reasons we eat dog meat. We believe it is very nutritious. It is especially good to strengthen the sick and those just out of the hospital. The Filipinos eat dog meat too.

When you were in our country, Mom, you learned about many of our Korean customs. Maybe they seemed strange to you. Koreans think there are strange customs in the United States too. What I think is what we are not used to, always is strange to us.

12

MUTUAL FRIENDSHIPS

This chapter is twofold. Stephen gives one of the "folds": "Mom, I want to talk about some people who are my very special friends. I met them at KNTC. That was a changing experience."

He thinks equally as much of his "special friends" in Manila and has already expressed the worth of their friendship to him and Grace. Several of his American friends, both in Korea and the Philippines, discuss their acquaintance with the Kims, Stephen's life of victory, and their mutual friendship. This is the second "fold."

"I met the Patches at KNTC," Stephen told me. "Bill Patch is the president of KNTC, and Gail Patch teaches English. They helped Grace and me in many, many ways. Mrs. Patch gave us American names. President Patch officiated at our wedding. He also helped us before that time. After we married, Gail Patch advised Grace about family planning—unusual, don't you think? They are both our friends and our spiritual parents. It is unusual in Korea to be both friends and parents, but it is possible with Americans."

"Yes, I gave Stephen and Grace their names," Gail Patch said. "They were in a special English class, and all were given Bible names. I chose 'Stephen' because he had suffered much and was a young man full of the Holy Spirit, like Stephen. I chose the name 'Grace" because that is what her Korean name, Hyung Suk, means. When they went to the seminary in Manila, all of the students were given Western names."

In 1990 the Patches visited with Stephen for a few minutes when he was in Korea to see what could be done for his eyes. The doctors gave him no hope. "He needed a hug," Gail said, "right there in McDonald's. In the States that would not be unusual, but it is in Korea. We joined hands and prayed that God would be with him and help him through this difficult time. We prayed that God would continue to help him to serve in the Philippines. We prayed that he would not become discouraged. Korean friends had told him he should say, 'Praise the Lord, I am suffering as my Lord suffered.' We told him that he didn't have to say, 'Praise the Lord, I am suffering,' but that God would like us to remember and rejoice.

"We said, 'Stephen, remember that you weren't expected to live when you had polio as a child. God healed you. Rejoice! Remember that the doctors said you would never be able to walk again. Your parents fasted and prayed and God healed you. Rejoice! Remember when you had that brain tumor and weren't expected to live. If you did, they said you would be a vegetable. God healed you. Rejoice!

"Stephen has a special anointing on his life. He has a heart for service. He has a love for missions and for others who are handicapped. He has felt a call to cross-cultural ministries and has taken the gospel light to the slums of Manila, to the mountain people of the Philippines, as well as to those in Baguio. Just as the Stephen in the New Testament church, he is 'a man full of God's grace and power and God has done great wonders and miraculous signs among the people' through Stephen Kim."

In 1983 the Kims met the Kenneth Pearsalls. Dr. Pearsall was the interim president of KNTC at that time. "We loved them with all our hearts," Stephen said, "and knew that they loved us. They are our other spiritual parents. We have received several letters from them since the earthquake occurred in Baguio. Their letters are always very, very sweet. They say, 'Stephen, how much we wish we were living near you so that we could bring you food and take care of you.' We know that they are really praying for us, and we are praying for them.

"After we came to the Philippines, they came to hold a preachers' meeting. Dr. Pearsall introduced me to President Fairbanks about being editor of the APNTS Newsletter. I was editor for two years.

"When they returned to the United States, the Pearsalls helped send a Work and Witness team from the Nampa College Church to build a dormitory. They sent us 82 hymnals for our church in Baguio."

Stephen told me that there were "so many beautiful stories between the Pearsalls and us." One of these is told by Kenneth Pearsall:

"When my assigned interpreter was unable to accompany me to Mokp'o one weekend, Steve was glad to travel with me as my 'mouthpiece' and to see his family again.

"The trip was delightful as Steve played his harmonica and sang some of his original compositions en route. Seeing the glad reunion with parents and siblings reinforced my impression of strong family love. It was a joy for me to hear Steve's vocal inflections parallel mine and observe his arm and hand point for emphasis even as I pointed or pounded. There was a kindred spirit superseding language barriers.

"It was apparent that Steve's Christian life was authentic among these folks who knew him best. Young people gathered around him as he smilingly reacted with them.

"Of course, we all know of Steve's severe physical problems in recent months. Despite pain, vision defects, and mounting financial burdens, Steve has given a clear testimony to God's adequacy in his life. He exemplifies the Prayer of Serenity."

"Also, I met you, Mom, at KNTC," Stephen said. "You know the stories about how we met and how we became close friends. And why now I am calling you 'Mom.' One thing that I remember well was in 1983 when I was a senior and we had a senior trip to Cheju Island. President Patch said you would be going with us. You were an old person in comparison with us, and at first we hesitated to have you join with us.

"We asked President Patch, 'What if she cannot travel and cannot walk very well?' But do you know what happened in Cheju-do? Wherever we went, you were always the first one who arrived at our point. You were really the strongest person among us. We were deeply impressed when we realized how strong you were."

Stephen talked about other missionaries, both in Korea and the Philippines, whose friendship he cherished. They cherished his also. Some of their comments follow.

"In preparation for summer ministries of the International Student Mission Corps [now Youth In Mission]," Tim Mercer wrote, "the faculty of KNTC selected four of our own Korean students to join the American students. One was Stephen Kim. His spirit, enthusiasm, and participation added vitality to the ministries of the team. Stephen's

Summer ministries with ISM'ers and KNTC students (Stephen, front row center).

confession at the end of those few weeks was 'Before this summer I thought that when God enabled me to walk, it was a great miracle. Now I realize that my salvation is an even greater miracle!'"

"Stephen has always been a survivor," wrote Roy Stults, who knew him both at KNTC and APNTS. "He not only has overcome many physical trials, but he has made them spiritual stepping-stones. They have not deterred him from doing doctoral work on the Old Testament or pastoring.

"He has always been zealous, hardworking, and diligent. He has been a leader both at KNTC and APNTS. An excellent student, Stephen has done well in learning English. Last year he did quite well in an extemporaneous sermon he gave in chapel at APNTS. Pastoring a church in the Philippines has refined his ability to work cross-culturally. He has always been able to relate well to 'foreigners' (foreigners to him).

"I know a number of things about Stephen. One thing I do *not* know about him is if he ever sleeps; I only see him in perpetual motion!"

Dr. George Rench's association with Stephen and letters of encouragement and helpfulness have already been seen. In addition he wrote, "I really appreciate Stephen and believe he is doing a superb job as the pastor of Baguio First Church. He has served faithfully and extremely effectively in a very difficult situation."

"Soon after my election as president of APNTS," wrote Dr. Fairbanks, "I met a young man with a big smile and a firm handshake, who introduced himself to me, 'I'm Kim Sung Kap, from Korea.' He really emphasized his country! 'American friends call me Stephen.'

"Stephen and Grace moved into a newly renovated apartment on campus. Though Stephen was crippled and had to walk approximately 35 steep steps from the administration building to his 'new' apartment, he never complained. He only expressed appreciation for the 'beautiful' facility in which he and his wife could live.

"Anne and I adopted a Korean child when he was nine months old. Our Stephen was nine years old when we moved to Manila. So very proud of his heritage, Stephen Kim spent time with our Stephen teaching him Korean words and customs.

"I have before me the Easter card Stephen prepared by himself," Dr. Fairbanks wrote from Mount Vernon Nazarene College. "It is beautiful. It included a beautiful photo of Stephen and his family in front of the church at Baguio City. His card spoke of recent revival services in the church. Stephen concluded his note to us with these words, 'The pain in my right foot reduced greatly through prayer, yet my eyes are still . . . agony!' He signed his letter 'From the shoulder of God.'"

Dr. Jim Edlin's comments about Stephen also speak of a close friendship. "Stephen Kim had a considerable impact upon our family. I felt that I knew Christ better because I had seen Him in Stephen. Certainly, it was Christ expressed through a culture different from my own, but it was unmistakenly the Christ of the Bible.

"What impacted me the most perhaps was Stephen's constant awareness of the reality of Christ in his life. It always seemed easy to talk about God and spiritual matters with him. He constantly and continually praised God through his words and actions. This life-style of constant praise seemed to me to be an intentional effort to express faith as well as to develop faith. And during the dark hours of the first brain tumor crisis, this life-style did not diminish.

"Somehow I sense that Stephen, like Jesus, would be willing to lay down his life for the sake of the salvation of others. Though he has so much to live for, I believe he would be willing to die for something even greater."

13

A CLOSING GLIMPSE

More than once when Stephen talked to me about his life, he referred to one of his "lives." He liked to think about what he called "my four lives." "My first life," he said, "was when I was a normal boy until I was three years old. My second life was that of a crippled boy. My third life was my handicapped life. My fourth life dates from my brain surgery."

Stephen is now in his "fifth life." A part of his wish expressed in a letter to the Fairbankses has been fulfilled: "I wish to see you again with a single vision and without pain." He is fleet of foot now, has 20/20 vision, and is entirely free from pain. Stephen is closer to his Lord than ever before, for he has been in His very presence since January 21, 1991. A brain tumor, larger and deeper than the first one, was his passport to heaven.

Equally fitting for his fifth life, as for his fourth, are Stephen's lines from *My Grace Is Sufficient for You:*

> I can see the light beyond this pain
> A brightened sea only I behold
> A smell of beautiful red rose
> A hopeful world in my hands!

"I haven't lived long, but God has allowed me to live much, much more." Stephen said this would be his answer to those who questioned a biography written about one so young. His 28 years were filled with the "much,

much more" of both joy and sadness. Now, his endless cycle of 28 years will be filled with only joy. Stephen's poem "Canvas" depicts not only those suffering, God-healing years but also, prophetically, his now-eternal ones:

Canvas

The last years of my canvas
Have been dark
Vegetable human being
Always the crutches
Right foot cannot deal
With sock's grasping power
Even for one day
Remove the pain Lord
My wife is pleading.

Another miracle
Out of my four lives
In my dream
Brother Elijah Kim
Laid his hands
And prayed for me
Not much pain left
I can deal with it.

Grace asked me
Where have you been
Are you really Stephen
Holding my hands
With tears
Hardly believing
Embracing her with all my heart.

Yes He will heal your eyes
Just like this instance
One morning
You will be standing like
A peaceful mountain
With normal eyes.

The pink color is
Appearing in my canvas
My dream will not end
I am satisfied
With this one day
I don't have to worry
About tomorrow
He will enable me
To live another day
That's why
One moment is even so precious
That's why I smile.

My canvas is being painted
Continually
The dark color has stopped
The bright color
Has filled in the canvas.

I am standing
At the end of this day
In order to paint
Another canvas.

Yes, Stephen, this canvas won't be landscapes and still lifes as much as you enjoyed painting them. Now, heaven's artist-in-residence, with an inspired brush you are painting "another canvas," the glories of the eternal . . .

May the glimpses we have caught of Stephen's earthly canvas painted brightly with faith, love, and devoted service inspire and challenge us all to live the more Excellent Way.

Stephen, Grace, Hei Jean, and Paul—Christmas 1990. Stephen died on January 21, 1991.